THE
GRACE
GATHERING

*The Communion of the Blessed
in a Broken World*

Gregory H. Sergent

Exploring Paul's Letter to the Ephesians

The Grace Gathering

© 2023
Gregory H. Sergent
ISBN 978-0-9966890-5-2
Soft Cover
All Rights Reserved

No part of this book may be reproduced or transmitted. in any form or by any means, electronic, including photocopying, recording, or any information storage system without permission in writing from the copyright owner.

Scripture References:

King James Bible for Today (KJBT)
King James Version (KJV)
New King James Version (NKJV)
New Living Translation (NLT)
English Standard Version (ESV)
Amplified Bible (AMP)

Credits

Cover Photo: Stan Crabtree
Editing: Reisa Sloce
Formatting & Publishing: Jim Cox

Hopeway Publishing
Gate City Virginia 24251
hopewaybooks.com

Dedicated

to the grace-filled people
of
Glamorgan Church
Wise, Virginia
and the memory of
those who have gone before us!

✞

*That in the ages to come he might
show the exceeding
riches of his grace
in his kindness toward us
through Christ Jesus.*

*For by grace you are saved
through faith;
and that not of yourselves;
it is the gift of God, not of works,
lest anyone should boast.*

~**The Apostle Paul**
Ephesian 2.4-9 (KJBT)

The Grace Gathering
A Communion of the Blessed in a Broken World

☩

Preface		1
Introduction		5

PART I
THE GRACE-FOCUSED PROCESS OF ASSIMILATION

Chapter One	The Gathering of the Broken	11
Chapter Two	A New Identity and Purpose	19
Chapter Three	The Ethos of a Healthy Church	31
Chapter Four	A Masterpiece in the Making	43
Chapter Five	The Cross-Formed Community	53
Chapter Six	Getting the Gospel Right	65
Chapter Seven	Praying for an Invasion of Love	77

PART II
THE GRACE-FILLED PRACTICE OF APPLICATION

Chapter Eight	Radical Love Lived-Out	85
Chapter Nine	The Anatomy of a Disciple	95
Chapter Ten	Uncommon Kindness	105
Chapter Eleven	The Subtle Slide into Sense-Driven Living	113
Chapter Twelve	The Incredible Life in the Spirit	123
Chapter Thirteen	The Sacred Alignment in Marriage	133
Chapter Fourteen	Survival Basics for the Family	143
Chapter Fifteen	Working Principles for the Workplace	155
Chapter Sixteen	Winning the War Within	163
Chapter Seventeen	Gathered for Genuine Care	175
Bibliography		183

*Receiving the Good News message
brings New Life to
those broken by sin and strife.*

*By faith, they form
a Communion of the Blessed—
a most
Gracious Gathering*

*Empowered through
Christ's Resurrected Life*

Preface

✚

Happiness and joy are in short supply today. Happy pursuits are often short-lived, and many are left disappointed with life. "If a man is the master of his destiny, then something has gone badly wrong." Our inclinations are correct!

The market for self-help books is a futile attempt to fix the problem. Personal trainers help those struggling with body image issues, and life coaches work on attitudes, tweak self-image, and help navigate life. Many feel unfulfilled and empty in their pursuit of self- actualization. Surface changes cannot alleviate deeper spiritual problems.

This sense of emptiness was similar to what Adam and Eve felt after their fall into sin. With guilt, shame, and fear, their life was never the same, and neither was their posterity. All humanity now realizes a certain spiritual death. Being deceived by the serpent and following his cues, they were in rebellion and an enemy of the Creator. An empty promise was their ultimate sense of self-realization, a life without the want or need of God.

In their broken relationship with God, they lost harmony and fellowship with their Creator. A dreadful curse of earthly toil, suffering, and death were the consequences upon them and their children. Yet God reached out in grace to them, as He has reached for us in saving grace. Some receive the gracious gift, while others become hardened in the rebellion. Like wandering stars, they become restless spirits searching and looking for rest. Without hope or satisfaction, their sad destiny is a "living death" without God and an ultimate eternal separation.

Without God's intervention, there is no possibility for personal restoration. The God who made man defines his purpose, establishes his destiny, and creates him for a harmonious communion with Himself. God continues a massive search and rescue of sinners for every generation. It is His gracious work.

God's manual for human satisfaction involves acknowledging Him as Creator and ongoing fellowship with Christ as our redeeming Savior. Jesus restores what's broken through the fall, a relationship with the Heavenly Father. The message of the good news is that Christ died for us while we were sinners, making reconciliation possible.

The church is the only institution in the world that explains the spiritual reason why people are so dissatisfied in life. The message of hope is that restoration is possible through Christ alone. He took our judgment for sin upon himself. The best possibility for any lasting human purpose is in the context of a relationship with Christ.

The church is the gathering of the broken, who have turned from sin and to Christ as Savior and Lord. The church's message is simple. Jesus is the Savior of sinners and the coming King of Glory! He will restore all things unto Himself. The church's message is Good News now and ultimately!

The perception of a modern and progressive culture is that the church's role is unnecessary, irrelevant, or even dangerous. Church attendance was once considered a privilege and priority of life. Personal preference is the new attitude today. Such nominal "Christianity" is neither salt nor light. The church is the context for a vibrant and growing spiritual life. It is in this context that personal spiritual growth happens. Paul's letter to Ephesians is for a specific people. But it is richly applicable to all people of faith.

We get a glimpse into Paul's heart for the church, the believer, and the importance of growing together in the body of Christ. The Apostles Paul and Peter declared the importance of understanding the believers standing in the Lord. Believers are God's people called out of darkness into the light. (cf. 1 Peter 2.9)

As we unpack the truths of Ephesians, read it thoroughly in several translations. Read aloud the text. It brings it to life. I appreciate the work of commentators and exegetes who help uncover the rich meaning of the Greek text. I hope to build upon their research.

I have interspersed pertinent background information throughout the chapters to bring insight for interpretation and application. I have added some Greek words for readers who prefer linguistic references for deeper study. A source bibliography is at the end for consideration. I pray that the applications rest solidly upon Scripture and fairly represent the source work of many gifted scholars. I fully own any deficiencies in handling the text.

May God help us understand the depth of His love and the reach of grace and mercy that brings the people of God together in gratitude for God and one another.

~Greg Sergent
New Year's Day 2023

The Epistle of Ephesians

Greetings 1:1-3

Grace-Focused Process of Assimilation

Being In Christ
Our Spiritual Blessings in Christ 1.1-14
Paul's Prayer for Spiritual Wisdom 1.15-22

Belonging to Christ Together
Made Alive & Raised up Together in Christ 2:1-9
Brought Near in Christ our Peace & Cornerstone 2.10-22

Becoming Christlike in Love
The Foundation of the Gospel 3. 1-9
Filled with the Fullness of Love 3.10-21

Grace-Filled Practical Application

A Sacred Walk unto Christ
In Unity as One 4.1-6
In Use of Spiritual Gifts 4.7-16
In Kindness 4.17-32
Imitating God 5.1-16

A Spirit Filled Walk
In Life 5.17-21
In Marriage 5.22-33
In Family 6.1-4
In Work 6.5-9

A Struggling Walk
Spiritual Armor 6.10-18
A Caring Community 6.19-22

Gracious Benedictions 6.12-24

Introduction

The Apostle Paul wrote two-thirds of the New Testament. Ephesians is packed with deep and extensive doctrinal truth and practical instruction in Christian living. Paul made mission trips to the commercial sea-port city of Ephesus in Asia Minor. He returned there to strengthen the disciples in the faith.

Ephesus had felt the sting of war and ruin, only to rebuild again to an even greater glory. It represented the best that the Roman Empire could offer. Ephesus was a city of vibrant commerce, education, and cultural diversity. Recovered from the ruins was a library. It boasted numerous writings supporting the schools, especially medicine. The Amphitheater was a center for civic activities and theatre and sporting events. Religious temples reveal ardent religious diversity and devotion. These stone-structured temples paled compared to the massive Temple of Artemis, one of the seven wonders of the ancient world.

The third-largest city, Ephesus, boasted the greatness of the Roman Empire. It was multi-ethnic, multi-religious, multi-cultural, among multiple world views. It was a city bustling with commerce in the marketplace and banking. Ephesus was a city that pursued pleasure. An overarching and cohesive factor in the Roman Empire was Caesar as "god among the gods." A massive statue of Domitian greeted entrants approaching the city from the sea.

PART I

THE GRACE-FOCUSED PROCESS OF ASSIMILATION

The Grace-Formed Community

A new society of Jews and Gentiles was budding amid this diverse environment. The centralized and cohesive element was not Greek philosophy or politics but the historical person of Jesus Christ as Savior from sin and Lord of life.

Being under house arrest, I imagine Paul's heart ached with longing as he penned this beloved letter. The gospel flourished amidst a panoply of religious expressions among the Greeks and Romans. The Good News that penetrated and changed the hearts of both Greeks and Jews brought these unlikely people groups together as one living body in Christ. They focused on the person of Jesus Christ, not their cultural and ethnic differences.

Aware of their cultural influences and at least the possibility of persecution, how could this socially diverse group of Jews and Greeks be unified in spreading the gospel? Paul had only one option–to strengthen the disciples. So, with quill and parchment and the support of a faithful colleague, Paul penned the letter to be hand-delivered by Tychicus.

All scholars agree that the letter has two parts: One dealing with essential doctrines of the faith in chapters 1-3 and the walk of faith in chapters 4-6. These general divisions were typical of Paul's writing style.

God's grace is the unifying theme of this circular letter. The unique kindness of God in Christ is the foundation of the new life of faith, community, and Christian practice. Review the quick overview of the outline presented on the previous page.

The Grace-Focused Process

Church leaders today strategize how to disciple people in Christ and into church life. They desire attendees to "embrace" the church's mission and vision. Assimilation is the buzzword among leaders today. I often wonder if people fully understand the core values and uniqueness of the church in the culture. What is the characteristic of a person who "gets it"? When does a passive spectator become active in church life? When does it happen?

I believe church attendees may be asking another set of correlating questions. Can God use me somewhere in His service? I want to feel I have a place where my uniqueness is valued. I want to belong. Yet, people struggle with feelings of inadequacy, guilt, fear, and unworthiness that stop them "dead in their tracks" before they would ever step out to serve. Many just don't feel worthy to serve.

I want to know that I am discovering my purpose and growing in the Lord through Bible-based teaching, a Christ-centered encounter in worship, and meaningful service. All of these are aspects of assimilation. These doctrinal chapters reveal a threefold process of assimilation: *being, belonging,* and *becoming.*

Assimilation

Paul provides the framework for church assimilation in the first three chapters.

Being

Chapter one deals with a stanza of three hymns, extolling the plan of the Father in verses 4-6 and His purpose in the Son in verses 7-12 through the power of the Holy Spirit. Chapter One addresses the issue of being in a relationship with the Father. It is a relationship based upon grace.

Paul desires that believers understand their unique standing "in Christ." The inward working of God's graces is the foundation of understanding who they are "in Christ," being fit for worship and belonging to this body of believers. Their spiritual blessing is being a new creation. Understanding their position "in Christ" is the firm footing for body life and becoming Christ-like.

Belonging

Paul addresses the problems associated with living in this world in Chapter Two. His day, much like our day, lacked an overarching unified vision or a worldview that explains the meaning of life and brings people together for a life of purpose.

Diverse people groups were called out of the dominion of Satan as children of disobedience, from a life of brokenness to one of blessed communion with Christ. In Christ, believers belong together. Uniquely called, the cross-formed community has a compelling message of peace and unity through the cross.

Becoming

In Chapter Three, Paul addresses the gospel as the apostolic witness. Their witness of Christ is the foundation of the church and the community growing in love.

The implications for worship in the first three chapters are poetic and theological. Paul segues into a beautiful, worshipful, and heartfelt prayer. He prays for the believers' growth in the depth of God's love. In this doctrinal section, he begins with a doxology and ends with a passionate pastoral appeal.

PART II

THE GRACE-FILLED PRACTICE OF APPLICATION

Paul packed massive doctrinal concepts in the first three chapters. But Paul was more than a philosopher, abstract theologian, or religious teacher. He was a pastor at heart–a theologian with "shoe leather." He desired that believers understand how to live out the Christian life.

Paul leans toward grace-filled living in ordinary places like marriage, home, work, and daily life. The practical instruction had far-reaching implications for believers trying to be faithful amid an immoral and hostile culture.

The Christian life is an ongoing work and life in the empowerment of the Holy Spirit. Believers stand in spiritual battles through spiritual armor. A caring church helps those with the pressure of spiritual battles.

Application

In a Sacred Walk

Applying the doctrines is a walk worthy of the Lord as one of unity in Chapter Four. Unity is worth protecting and nurturing. It is such a radical love that lives out the grace extended in word and deed, imitating the very nature of the God of grace.

A Spirit-Filled Walk

Chapter Five is a pivotal chapter where Paul describes this new walk empowered by the Holy Spirit. The Spirit of God's fullness indwells believers, enabling them to a new life of submission to Christ's Lordship in a unified love. Paul's understanding is that the new life under the Holy Spirit is the life of the grace gathering in the home, family, and workplace.

A Struggling Walk

Paul is not dismissive concerning the struggles and conflicts we face. He recognized that the real battle was spiritual wickedness in high places among principalities and powers, motivated by the prince and the power of the air. Believers need spiritual armor and the healing salve of compassionate grace in caring for the wounded.

A Unique Gathering

The church is the most unique institution on earth! The life of God is on display through gracious kindness. Such a community is attractive to those looking from the outside. A healthy church is rare compared to the organized social structures in the larger society.

The depth of the purest love flows from the heart of God's grace through His people. The heavenly Father catches the broken soul from its free fall toward destruction. Such a grace is worth celebrating and exploring. Let's discover the depth of such grace on full display in the Grace Gathering.

*Blessed be the God and Father of our Lord
Jesus Christ, who has blessed us with all
spiritual blessings in heavenly places
in Christ:*

*According as he has chosen us in him
before the foundation of the world,
that we should be holy
and without blame before him
in love:*

*Having predestined us unto the adoption
of children by Jesus Christ to himself,
according to the good pleasure
of his will,*

*To the praise of the glory
of his grace, in which he has
made us accepted
in the beloved.*

Ephesians 1.1-6 (KJBT)

A Gathering of the Broken

Chapter One

Ephesians 1.1-3

There has never been a time in human history when people have been more connected. Our phones and the internet bring the world to our fingertips, yet people feel isolated and lack meaningful relationships. Basic family units are hurting and broken. Feelings of rejection, alienation, and not "belonging" are an emotional stronghold for many wounded hearts.

The post-modern mood is pervasively *cynical* about everything from relationships to life issues. Wallowing in disappointment, many conclude that hypocrisy is prevalent, authentic community is a lie, and life meaning happens on the cuff. The message is clear: you live for now and make it up as you go.

A pervasive and invasive media influence reinforces the message through images and slick marketing that "you don't match up with unless" or "you are missing out on" what matters now. Regardless, the message is easily internalized and feeds feelings of rejection.

Broken & Fragmented

Massive information dumps overload the mind and emotions. People feel more overwhelmed with life than ever. It feels like it's flying apart at the seams or holding on by a thread. The weakening of life around us leaves many feeling insecure. Life just feels like it's unraveling into chaos!

The fragmentation we see on a social level mirrors deeper spiritual issues. Alienation from God is at the heart of the soul fractures. Spiritual bankruptcy and death are the conditions of hearts without Christ. People are ever grasping but never reaching inward wholeness. This wholeness only happens in "communion" with God and requires His intervention.

Humans long for a sense of community. We seek it and search it out. Christian fellowship and community are both immensely fulfilling. There is great joy in such an authentic community, but it is also a source of deep pain when it breaks down. We can know God and peace and live peacefully with one another. That's why Jesus left the "wholeness" of heaven to walk on broken streets. He attracted broken people who needed rescue from sin and restoration in life. The church has been gathered from the broken fragments of this world and called to wholeness.

As you work through the pages of the Grace Gathering, I pray you will embrace Christ's forgiveness and release from sin's bondage. He will create within you a new heart shaped by His grace and acceptance of you. The "hole" in your life can be transformed into "wholeness" in Christ! Such a transformation is radically life-changing!

The Grace Gathering

Paul planted the church in Ephesus during a time of social fragmentation. Strife and conflict characterized relationships between both Greeks and Jews. People of the empire felt the intimidation from Rome's heavy-handed attempt to build social cohesion. God planted His people in such a context, and the gospel flourished.

Believer's new identity in Christ was the basis of their belonging in this. new kingdom community. It is astounding, if not miraculous, that such a community could survive in such a cultural climate. The gathering of unlikely people groups around the person of Jesus Christ and the good news was the social cohesion of broken ones made whole.

A Gathering of the Blessed

Paul writes a typical letter identifying himself as an apostle of Jesus Christ, addressed to the saints and faithful in Christ. Grace and peace are usual Pauline greetings with trinitarian doctrinal inferences.

Paul addresses his apostolic calling to the faithful (vs. 1-2), the commitment of faithful saints (vs. 2), and the community of the blessed in the salutation. His greeting models God's kindness.

> Paul, an apostle of Jesus Christ by the will of God, to the saints who are at Ephesus, and to the faithful in Christ Jesus: Grace be to you, and peace, from God our Father, and from the Lord Jesus Christ. Blessed be the God and Father of our Lord Jesus Christ, who has blessed us with all spiritual blessings in heavenly places in Christ:
> (Ephesians 1.1-3, KJBT)

Addressing numerous house churches, Paul reminds the saints that God calls together a community of grace and peace.

Called unto Christ

Those called by God's grace can live "whole" in a world of brokenness. God's grace at work through them is a beautiful display of the grandeur of God. The life of Paul is such an example of God's gracious work. Paul was the self-professed chief of sinners. The apostle realized his calling freed him from sin's penalty and power. He abandoned trusting in his performance in keeping the law for his righteousness! He was now trusting Christ's perfect righteousness as the law keeper. The glorious, good news was his message that would go into the world.

What a change! Saul of Tarsus was now Paul the Apostle to the Gentiles. His life radically changed. With calling *klesis* in the New Testament comes the idea of receiving an invitation to a banquet. God's invitation to receive the good news is an invitation for communion with Christ.

Paul stands as a model of a Christ-centered life and a grace-filled message. Being called from among the prestigious religious elite of his day, Paul was now a humble "bondservant" *doulos* of Christ. *(cf.* Romans 1.1) He had given up all rights to Christ. His new identity was through the all-sufficient work of Christ, not his religious duty or moral obligation. His new role was an ambassador of the gospel to the whole world.

Are you connected with your calling? Such a life connects you with your eternal purpose. It is a most satisfying fellowship with Christ. It simplifies life and guides you into a glorious future. The gathering of the blessed live wholeheartedly for an audience of one—the God of all grace!

Committed to Faithfulness

Faithfulness is a worthy goal of every believer. God has not called us to be famous, well-known, or influential. God has not even called us to make an impact. He has called us to be obedient to Christ, passionate in worship, and our life poured out as a living sacrifice to Christ.

No other person exemplified this more than the woman who broke open the bottle of fragrant oil and anointed Jesus. It was that fragrance that accompanied Jesus to the cross. It is the fragrance of adoration and obedience. Her one act of kindness left an indelible mark on human history.

Paul identifies the believers in Ephesus as saints. They were the set-apart ones unto the Lord. In a city committed to the best the culture could offer, believers were positioned as "holy" before the Lord and wholly obedient to Christ. Faithfulness in doctrine and lifestyle characterized his life. Being faithful means living like Jesus among the broken, being His hands and feet. We bring Jesus' life to the broken.

Grace & Peace

Grace & Peace – the typical greeting of Paul is also the unique character of the church. Grace *charis* is a prominent theme found 13 times in this epistle. The gracious kindness of God is the gift of salvation received and lived out. It firmly rests in God's favor and His kingdom operation on earth.

In a harsh and unkind world, the unified church displays gracious kindness in word and deed. Jesus prayed for the church in this regard. The world needs to know the Father.

> I am in them, and you are in me. May they experience such perfect unity that the world will know that you sent me and that you love them as much as you love me.
> (John 17.23, NLT)

A mentor and Bible teacher, James Cox defines grace as:

"The kindness of God shown to sinners, resulting in the power of God being exercised on behalf of sinners."

The power of such gracious kindness lives out in peace. *Shalom* is a Hebraic greeting of good wishes. Peace *eirene* in Greek describes it as an inner calm. So, the new community of faith is a healthy, peace-filled environment that pursues peace with everyone. It is being at peace with God and abiding in the peace of God daily.

First-century Ephesus was immoral, unjust, and filled with tension and conflicts–politically, socially, and racially. They had rebuilt from a bitter, war-torn past. There were ongoing tensions between Jews and Greeks. They were far from being anything, either healthy or calm. As mentioned earlier, social strife only reflects the unrest within the human condition.

Peace is counter-cultural in a chaotic world. It always is. Jesus, the Prince of Peace, is also the author of peace. He brings inner calm and a community that rests securely in Him. Christ is their new identity as the center of the community. Jesus will one day reign in peace as Lord at the consummation of human history. So, the church's compelling testimony today is not about her perfection but the goodness of God through Christ's perfect work. Jesus said the "gates of hell will not prevail" against the church. Why? Jesus does not fail, and neither does the gospel of Christ!

Blessing the Lord

The gathering is blessed "in Christ"! Paul describes the sphere and operation of these blessings. They are spiritual and operative through the Holy Spirit. Through His resurrection and ascension, He is seated in the place of authority, and believers are "seated" with Him in heavenly places. We live out heaven's blessings in the real world.

Christ is the ultimate authority as ruler. He is Lord over all nations, kingdoms, and realms, seen and unseen, in heaven and earth. The believer's identity and authority are "in Christ." Christ takes bitter and broken lives and makes them into the "communion of saints" who bless the Lord.

In Heavenly Places

Our enlightenment age denies much of anything unseen and scientifically unmeasurable. Paul describes a spiritual realm where Christ rules over all principalities and powers, material and immaterial, seen and unseen. The implications are that believers can fully trust Christ.

The believer's blessing is indeed heavenly. The unseen spiritual realm influences happenings on earth. Paul teases this out in the epistle. The ancients understood that their world included the operation of good and evil spiritual entities.

In heavenly places, Christ is seated in spiritual authority far above all principalities, powers, and dominions for all time. (1.3, 20-21) The believer is raised with Christ and seated together with Him. As such, believers are fellow citizens (2.19), fitted and built together in love (2.21-22), partakers together (3.6), unified in the Spirit (4.3), the body of Christ (4.13), members of His body (5.30), and believers who make supplication for all the saints (6.18). Are you getting the picture? Christ is Lord, and we are seated with Him.

In this authoritative position, the multifaceted wisdom of God is displayed in the church to principalities and powers (3.10-11). Paul finally reveals the believers' real battle is the spiritual conflict in heavenly places and with the rulers of spiritual darkness in this present age (6.12). So, the kingdom of light shines brightly in a world held captive by the domain of darkness. Their message was God's great kindness extended through Christ to all who repent of sin and trust Him. The church is the heaven-authorized and grace-filled community formed among those born anew into God's gracious kingdom.

Bless the Lord

What could happen if our prayers focused on praising God for His provisions? The earmark of the gathered community is praise. The church blesses the Lord.

Looking at this prison epistle of Paul, I am amazed that Paul only briefly mentions the details of his containment. He does not recap his miserable situation or lodge extensive complaints about the circumstances. On the contrary, he begins the chapter with a doxology.

Ten verses are one continuous exhortation in the Greek language. Paul intended to praise the Father for His wisdom, Christ's provision in salvation, and the Holy Spirit's work in bringing this salvation to completion.

What if our prayers shifted from asking for God's blessing to a joyous celebration of blessing the Lord? We must not give place to the Evil One by complaining. Complaining about circumstances, people, our present needs, or even the world situation only magnifies the source of the conflict.

Adoration and praise of God break spiritual strongholds! Your adoration of the Lord is your invitation for heaven to go to work in the present issues. So, begin blessing the Lord and see what God begins to do in your life. You might find yourself surprised by His ongoing kindness at work.

Conclusion

In this new community, the broken gather to praise and magnify the worthiness of Christ. They choose to see the goodness of God in a weary and worn-out world. It seems strange to this world, but it is heaven's reality on earth. The Grace Gathering is complete in Christ, and He is our ultimate, all-sufficient source of satisfaction. Praise and gratitude are attractive.

No matter the brokenness, God uses cracked pots and makes them whole in Christ. Christ specializes in gathering a community of the broken as a blessed community called to the praise of His glory!

Grace

✠

"The kindness of God shown to sinners, resulting in the power of God being exercised on behalf of sinners."
~Jim Cox

Amazing grace how sweet the sound
That saved a wretch like me
I once was lost, but now I'm found
Was blind but now I see

'Twas grace that taught my heart to fear
And grace my fears relieved
How precious did that grace appear
The hour I first believed

Through many dangers, toils, and snares
I have already come
This grace that brought me safe thus far
And grace will lead me home

When we've been here ten thousand years
Bright, shining as the sun
We've no less days to sing God's praise
Than when we first begun

~John Newton

A New Identity & Purpose

Chapter Two

Ephesians 1.4-14

What an exciting time to be alive. Massive amounts of information are at our fingertips. I was recently awe-struck by the images of our solar system taken from the lens of powerful space telescopes. My understanding is that we get glimpses of the universe from light-years away. Frankly, I can hardly wrap my mind around the concept, yet the reality remains that our universe is vast, beautiful, colorful, ordered, complex, and mysterious. It struck awe and wonder within me!

With every new bit of information, our knowledge about the planet and our place on it increases. These scientific pursuits lead to asking questions about man's purpose and meaning. Scientific endeavors slip into questions of philosophy. These are the deeper inclinations within the human experience toward self-discovery. As a teenager in the 1970's *me-generation*, I remember hearing people say, I just need to get away to find myself. What they were saying was that something was missing in the human experience. *I Can't Get No Satisfaction* was the song of the era.

Such an internal quest spawned the self-help genre in bookstores. From New Age spirituality to pop psychology filled the airways on talk shows. Self-discovery came of age in the 1980s. Who doesn't have a vested interest in themselves? Looking within for answers was the theme in popular movies in these postmodern times. It was one more vain attempt of people in search of meaning.

People just seem more confused today. What a paradox with such knowledge at our disposal. The problem is we carelessly head off in empty directions with grand hopes of fulfilling perceived needs. No wonder many live in perpetual disappointment and eventual disillusionment. Cynical attitudes are pervasive and a dread of the future. Superficial pursuits in religion, morality, or spirituality cannot fix what remains broken in the human heart. There must be more to life. There is!

Hidden in Plain Sight

Our internal inclinations for hope are correct. Being motivated in the search for life's meaning, man's internal compass points to God. God is often the last place many want to go or turn. Rightfully so, we recognize that we must give up our self-pursuit. Many just continue in self-pursuits, remaining locked in a miserable pool of introspecttion. Unfortunately, many people have written off a relationship with Christ altogether. Perhaps it is out of gross misconceptions about God or flat-out rebellion against Him. The latter is true most often, I suspect.

Morbid introspection neither cleanses nor satisfies the soul. Being in a relationship with Christ settles the question of *who I am and why I am here.* Being in a relationship with Christ settles the question of who I am and why I am here. God's fingerprints are all around us and even within us. His steps are before us in the person of Jesus Christ! Our life in Christ has discovered purpose and satisfaction in communion with God in the grace-gathered community. Surprised by love and joy, God was there the whole time– hidden in plain sight.

Our Identity in Christ

I have been honored with the soul care of people for forty years now as a pastor. I delight and love the uniqueness of people. I have observed that many faith struggles are spiritually connected to how people see themselves. How people view themselves is the result of how they view God. These are thoroughly interconnected realities, along with our worship. The good news is our rescue to be embraced and grow in.

When we see God as He is–Holy, we see ourselves as sinful and separated from Him. We gain a new identity and become God's child through receiving Christ by faith. It's like God cleanses the lens of our spiritual eyes and aligns our hearts to His intended purpose for us.

This discovery began for me as a teenager. One summer evening in 1976, I acknowledged that my feeble attempts for self-sufficiency and satisfaction were failing miserably. I surmised that my moral goodness was good enough for God. It was not until I recognized that I desperately needed Christ's rescue and forgiveness of sin that my life changed.

My identity centered on being popular among peers, desperately wanting their acceptance, and feeling loved. I had mental images I'd seen in magazines or on television that shaped who I wanted "to be and become". It was image-driven idolatry! I needed forgiveness, but I had no idea how God's acceptance would free me to live for His approval alone. When my heart became open to the Savior's compelling call, a personal breakthrough followed.

Religion or Relationship

Paul was addressing a culture that understood religious devotion. The Greeks would choose their gods from a panoply of gods. People appealed to the pagan gods for their personal needs. This involved rituals, incantations, ecstatic experiences, sacrifices, and even oracles as prescribed by temple priests and priestesses.

The Graeco-Roman gods were capricious, fickle, easily offended, and manipulated. People attempted to gain their favor and help. Like the Greeks, our sophisticated, self-made gods appealed to transacting for personal fulfillment. We look at religion as a transaction rather than a relationship.

The gods of the Ephesians were untrustworthy. They were cold and unpredictable in their appeasement. In contrast, Paul reveals that the Heavenly Father is seated in sovereignty, wisdom, and prudence filled with love for His children. He acts in gracious favor through the purest motivation of love *agape*. Herein lies the uniqueness of biblical Christianity among the world of religions. The nature of God is personal and relational.

These key relational concepts, Paul describes as spiritual blessings in Christ. These are heavenly blessings flowing from God the Father, purchased by God the Son through the power of God the Holy Spirit.

> According as he has chosen us in him before the foundation of the world, that we should be holy and without blame before him in love: Having predestined us unto the adoption of children by Jesus Christ to himself, according to the good pleasure of his will, To

> the praise of the glory of his grace, in which he has made us accepted in the beloved. (Ephesians 1. 4-6, KJBT)

Carefully and thoughtfully consider the magnitude of these many spiritual blessings in your relationship with Christ. Thoughtfully pray that your mind conforms to this heavenly reality. Embracing these truths will help shape how you view yourself, God, life in general, and particularly worship. It's a real-life changer here and now!

The Father's Loving-kindness

For those born from above, He is a loving Heavenly Father. God is both *personal* and *relational*. His divine attributes are omniscience, omnipresence, omnipotence, holiness, and love, and He executes providential care over His you. He sustains and guides His children.

God's choosing is best interpreted and understood in terms of His relational nature. He thoroughly knows us from beginning to end. In His foreknowledge, He is not surprised by what happens on earth. The sands of time sift through his providential hands. He acts in providential care by calling sinners unto himself in repentance.

God desires that you know Him in a personal and loving relationship. He wants you to belong to His heavenly family. God desires communion with you and extends an invitation for any who will receive and believe by trusting Christ through faith. You were in God's thoughts since the world's foundations. He sent His Son to pay for your sin. The Holy Spirit draws you to Christ for salvation.

Being Chosen

The Hebrews were chosen as God's special people to bear the covenant blessing of Abraham and hence be a blessing to all the nations of the earth. The church is a chosen generation, royal priesthood, and holy nation. Our identity leads to purposeful doxology being "called forth the praises of God." (cf. 1 Peter 2.9)

Therefore, believers are the elect in Christ. Election does not rest upon personal merit, work, or a perceived foreseen goodness within you. It is motivated by the loving-kindness of the Father (cf. 2 Timothy 1.9). He calls sinners from the world's slave market of sin and chooses them as his covenant family in love. Salvation is from the Lord, extended as a gift to be received.

Chosen *eklego* means to pick or be chosen out for oneself (vs.14). God foreknows believers chosen "in Christ" to be holy and without blame. Denoting the believer's new standing, they are the righteousness of God in Christ. He forgives their guilt and gives Christ's righteousness unto them. They have a firm footing to step forward as holy before the Lord.

This holy standing is the foundation for right living in the world. Very similarly, Paul uses the term justification in Romans. Believers are declared right before the Father. This judicial act of God renders believers in Christ free from the penalty of guilt. The believer is declared holy.

The believer is without blame before the Father. The believer is faultless and unblemished because of the work of Christ in salvation. Upon Jesus was laid the charges of our sin. In a moral sense, Jesus was faultless, but Jesus bore the fault of our sins as our substitute legally. Jesus carried the weight of our sin!

Pause and let this truth sink in deeply. The Heavenly Father thoroughly knows your life. He is neither surprised nor shocked at your failures, sins, mishaps, regrets, feelings of guilt, and shame. These are the areas where we find ourselves tripped up in spiritual defeat and trapped in a cycle of self-rejection. Christ provides us with a righteous standing before God. But the news is even greater. We have a glorious future awaiting us.

The Heavenly Father is committed to loving you because His nature is love. He cannot do anything but love. His love compels a choice to reciprocate that love in praise, devotion, obedience, and service! We love Him because He first loved us.

Being Adopted & Accepted

Paul understands God's providential activity in adoption and accepting believers in Christ. Believers become members of God's family. Predestination is a related term referenced a few times in Scripture, mainly in the books of Ephesians and Romans. It means to decide beforehand or to pre-determine. It's more than a term for theological debate, as it has been for over 500 years. It has rich implications when internalized for believers.

Being predetermined by the astrological alignment of the stars, many appealed to Artemis to change one's fate. Stoics resigned that "whatever will be will be" and best left to the gods. But there was never any sense of security when transacting with the fickle gods. It was a dreadful religious fatalism indeed.

Even today, scientific atheism holds a similar fateful worldview. One's choices and destiny are encoded in his DNA. They surmise that man's behavior and life are predetermined and written in his biology. Man is dancing to his physiological make-up and bears no responsibility for his choices.

Being Predestined in Christ

What does Paul mean by predestination? Is Paul describing a cause-effect model for understanding God, much like scientific observation? Is he advocating a sanctified form of Stoicism where man is simply living out a drama of the gods? Is man only a robot in his behavior and life, with his choices being driven by the physical? Neither of these represents the nature of God as providentially caring in a personal relationship.

God's *relational* and *personal* nature is the best lens for understanding predestination. God *Elohim* created the world by His spoken word. He causes through speaking, and the effect is material creation. God created man from the material creation of earth and breathed into him, and man became a living soul. God created man with personhood and personality. In Genesis chapter 2, we find that the term used for God was Yahweh, bearing his covenant name. Covenant implies a relationship.

He created Adam and Eve in terms of relationship. He had communion with them. The conventional term was obedience as evidence of a relationship of love. The late Leroy Forlines offers a theological construct that is insightful and helpful. Rather than a cause-effect model for understanding God's work in salvation, Forlines suggests a plausible influence-response model that considers God's sovereignty in personal and relational terms. It is in keeping with His nature and displays our capacity for relationship.

Man is not a puppet on a string. God has sovereignly designed relationships where the free expression of human choice is actual. A person can either receive God's appeal of grace or willingly reject God's offer. Through the enabling draw of the Holy Spirit, man may receive God's gift of salvation or reject the divine influences of grace. God is sovereign in the influence-response model.

This explanation allows the natural, built-in tension of the existence of God's sovereignty and man's will. Being in Christ, the believer's predetermined destiny involves conformity to Christ. God foreknows all who actually will believe. (cf. Romans 8.30) On the same token, the beloved Apostle John reminds believers that God so loved the world that He gave his only begotten son that whosoever believes in him should not perish but have everlasting life. (cf. John 3.16)

The gospel of Christ that is heard appeals to the mind and heart to be received. As many who receive him become the children of God. In essence, God has predetermined that salvation is in Christ and makes the offer to whosoever will. Becoming the elect happens only in Christ, through receiving the all-sufficient work of Christ by faith. Salvation is within the context of a relationship.

The believer in Christ is called and adopted as His child and accepted because of the gracious kindness of the Heavenly Father. Predestination should not be a concept that strikes images of a dreadful, fate-filled destiny, but more like the compelling draw of an open-armed Father awaiting his child to fall fully and completely into His loving embrace. The broken are no longer estranged, alienated, or rejected. Even Gentiles are elect through the riches of God's grace.

I find great comfort in the relational understanding because it reveals the mysterious depths of the counsels of God in His work of salvation and the spreading of the gospel in the larger world. Being in Christ, the believer views himself differently. Feelings of self-rejection, inadequacy, and not belonging can change through understanding this truth. Feelings change through conforming our thinking to our new position in Christ.

We are members of His family full of praise and blessing. It is the ultimate acceptance based upon His love. Believers then can enjoy God in such a relationship and will enjoy Him forever. It is a cause for praise.

Bible doctrine is the foundation for Christian worship. Worship and service is your purpose for living.

Christ's All-Sufficient Provision

Believers in Christ have redemption and forgiveness and gather as one in Christ. Three glorious concepts are central to understanding the work of Christ in salvation. Christ's all-sufficient provision in redemption rests in the Sovereign counsel of God's revealed will.

> In whom we have redemption through his blood, the forgiveness of sins, according to the riches of his grace; In which he has abounded toward us in all wisdom and prudence; Having made known unto us the mystery of his will, according to his good pleasure which he has purposed in himself: That in the dispensation of the fullness of times he might gather together in one all things in Christ, both which are in heaven, and which are on earth; even in him:
> (Ephesians 1.7-10, KJBT)

Jesus' sacrifice was provided upon the cross by the will of God and his great love and provision of salvation for all humanity, regardless of ethnicity or social status. Christ's sacrifice for salvation provides for everyone, but it only effectively works in those with faith in Christ.

Redemption

Paul utilizes a strong imagery of slaves bought off the slave market and freed. The clear message is the believer's freedom from the powerful bondage of sin rests upon Christ. Through Jesus' death on the cross, the power of sin is crushed and broken, and the glorious resurrection of Jesus makes us righteous before God.

Slavery was the economic system in the Roman Empire. Many people were slaves and could buy their freedom out of slavery. The believer purchased from sin's slave market emancipated to serve a new master–Christ. Christ is the great liberator for those in the bondage of sin.

Forgiven

It is genuinely good news when the believer receives Christ's perfect work on the cross as all-sufficient for the forgiveness of sin. Being released from the penalty and power of sin, believers can move forward as a new creation in Christ. There is release and new beginnings to be received.

Forgiveness is such a massive topic, more than can be addressed here. Without a relationship with Christ, man is guilty before God, but in Christ, man finds forgiveness. Past sins and condemnation are a forgiveness to embrace and stand upon. There is no condemnation for those who walk in faith. Christ's work is sufficient to forgive your sin and secure your future.

Gathered Together

So, the new community of faith in Jesus gathered as one. All things are coming together in heaven and earth in Christ. God's wisdom and prudence reveal the mystery of God's will in Christ. It is a rich grace lavished on believers. It's on display like a brilliant diamond's reflection of light. Paul simply said that this grace abounded toward us.

Such overflowing grace is by His good pleasure to the praise of His glory. Why? Because God's nature is gracious kindness. What a glorious salvation for the believer's praise! God created us to know and be recipients of this heavenly blessing of salvation.

The Spirit's Power & Presence

So, these passages show us that the work God did beforehand is a present possession deposited within believers. It will also be a future reality, all things wrapped in God's eternal nature.

Inheritance

We have received a grand inheritance from the Father. It is the outworking of His will accomplished through the operation of the Holy Spirit. The Spirit places a deposit of His presence within the believer.

> In whom we have also obtained an inheritance, being predestined according to the purpose of him who works all things after the counsel of his own will: That we who first trusted in Christ should be to the praise of his glory. In whom you also trusted, after you heard the word of truth, the gospel of your salvation: in whom also after you believed, you were sealed with the Holy Spirit of promise, who is the down payment on our inheritance until the redemption of the purchased possession, unto the praise of his glory. (Ephesians 1.13-14, KJBT)

We are God's purchased possession, belonging to God and the new faith community. In salvation, the Holy Spirit seals and officially authenticates the believer's new standing. James Cox describes the seal as proof of a finished transaction that has been fully satisfied with the official verification of ownership.[1] The Holy Spirit is the down payment that verifies the penalty of sin that is fully satisfied and will one day be fully redeemed, delivering the believer from the presence of sin.

Believers have a glorious standing and await a future glorification. The cross of Christ is God's reversal of sin' curse. The resurrection of Jesus proves that sin's power is broken and eradicated one day. No wonder Paul blesses the Lord, and so should we.

Conclusion

Can you imagine how unique such a community was in the Roman Empire? A community of gratitude and praise for unseen spiritual blessings. These glorious, heavenly trues shape the believer's lives on earth. Paul encourages hearts to praise and walk in the reality of Christ's glory! It was enough for Paul to break forth in praise. It should be enough for us to break forth in a joyous chorus of praise.

We are neither deserving nor entitled to such grace. We are only humble recipients. Have you received such a grace that offers a new standing? How are these truths influencing your worship? Awe and gratitude are the proper response to such a marvelous and rich grace.

---

[1] James Glen Cox, Spiritual Blessings from Your Heavenly Father, Hopeway Publishers, Gate City, 2021, 54-55.

Let these truths settle deeply in your heart. Let this shape your thinking, how you feel about God, and how you live out your faith. Like Paul's doxology in chapter one, ascribes glory-*doxa* to God that He rightfully deserves.

We are created and compelled to revel in the celebration of Christ! Nothing fuels that celebration like counting the innumerable blessings listed in Ephesians 1. These blessings are like the fragrant perfume poured out upon Jesus. God delights in the fragrant lives of His grace-gathered people. So, put on the garments of praise and break open your bottle of lavish praise. Proclaim His marvelous grace. It is light and hope for a broken world!

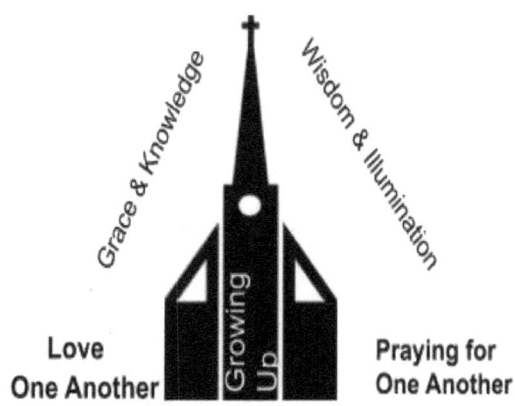

The Ethos of a Healthy Church

Chapter Three

Ephesians 1.15-23

Forefront in the thinking of most Americans is physical health. Concerns for aging, stress, obesity, issues of nutrition, exercise, rest, prevention, and supplements are topics of interest for many. The message is clear. The key to a quality life is a healthy lifestyle, especially heart health.

I enjoyed weekly Monday morning meetings with a small group of pastors at McDonald's for several years. We jokingly called our meeting McChurch. It was our "post-game" follow-up from Sunday services. We'd share stories, sermon thoughts, service details, frustrations, and even heartaches. We discovered that "every pastor needs a pastor" for support, encouragement, and a listening ear. Their support has encouraged me as a pastor. They are some of my dearest friends.

God has uniquely designed our lives for communion with Him and community with one another. No one is an island to themselves, and we become stronger through fellowship when the walls of isolation crumble.

The evidence is clear that the heartbeat of a vibrant faith community is healthy relationships. Drawing crowds of people to church is much easier and faster than forming deep and lasting relationships. Yet these deep friendships help people grow in Christ and handle their troubles.

As a pastor, I have had the privilege of observing the church go into action in ministry. From helping navigate issues in marriage, dealing with rebellious children, and coping with anxiety, stress, grief, and heart-wrenching situations, a caring church is beautiful as Christ's light and love. The world takes notice!

Our quick-fix culture demands attending to life's heartaches and seeking resolution immediately. A grace-gathered congregation does not settle for conformity to outward styles or "quick fixes" as adequate markers of church health. Growing in Christ is a deeper conformity of the soul and spirit to Christ. It is an ongoing process that only happens in the context of a healthy church. It is slow, painstaking, and sometimes messy. How does a church create an environment where people are nurtured and growing in Christ through some of their darkest times? Paul gives us great insight in verses 15-23.

> Therefore, I also, after I heard of your faith in the Lord Jesus, and love unto all the saints, do not cease to give thanks for you, making mention of you in my prayers;
> (Ephesians 1.15-16, KJBT)

Paul understood that the *ethos* of a healthy church environment is attractive to people. Hearing the gospel and doctrine taught and applied is essential. Engaging Christ-centered worship is encouraging and ministers to the heart. Christ is the focus of our worship, friendships, and service opportunities in the church and the world. These are at least a few essential elements for church health.

The Ethos of a Healthy Church

Ethos describes the character or what makes up a family or community. We would call it the core values defining the essence of a culture, nation, community, or even a church. What were the characteristics of these Ephesian house churches as a grace-gathered community?

A Growing Faith in Christ

Therefore, I also, after I heard of your faith in the Lord Jesus and your love for all the saints, vs. 15.

The first-century church had a unique and exclusive worldview. The Christian worldview did not add Jesus to the pantheon of gods in Greek culture. Remember, Christianity emerged out of Judaism. Jesus was the fulfillment of Old Testament prophecies. Jesus was the way, the truth, and the source of life, exclusively the Lord. Paul received the welcomed news that believers were strengthening in the gospel of Christ. The apostles were dedicated to faithful teaching and equipping the saints.

Their faith was a firm conviction. It yielded a certainty based on orthodox beliefs. It was not a nominal adherence to a belief system or a vague esoteric feeling. It was nothing like pagan temple worship and practice. Believers embraced the objective truth of the gospel. Their spiritual aspiration was a desire to live faithfully for Christ. For many, this meant being misunderstood and ostracized by family or friends. Some faced exclusion from the marketplace for failing to give Caesar homage as lord.

Their faith was scrutinized and tried in a tumultuous culture of rampant immorality. The church valued surrendering to Christ as Lord, regardless of the cost.

Where is the foundation of your faith? We often misplace our faith by trusting family traditions, fleeting emotional experiences, ethical systems, or pleasant circumstances. Is your faith firmly anchored in a growing relationship with Christ? Are you resting fully in the truth claims of Scripture and the sufficiency of Christ? Is your faith in Christ a firm and settled conviction, no matter the circumstance?

Love for all the Saints

Our busy lives hinder us from making deeper friendships. We are constantly on the go! We become stressed out with our schedules stretched to the limits. Sadly, gathering for church might feel like one more demand. It is easy to treat the gathering as optional. The church calls us from busy activities to building relationships for eternity's sake. It takes time, intention, and personal sacrifice.

Sometimes we think of church life as buildings, ornamentations, and external programs. The house churches of Ephesus lacked such trappings. Church was the people gathered around the person of Christ. A love for Christ, His word, and love for fellow believers was the *ethos* of the early church. The social cohesion of the fellowship was a sacrificial love for one another. Their unique identity was as God's family on earth.

Prayers for One Another

Paul had a deep affection for the people within the churches. Being confined through Roman house arrest did not hinder his pastoral concern. It only modified his ministry. Paul did not *cease to give thanks, making mention in prayers.* He prayed for Christ's ongoing work among them.

His heart overflowed with thanksgiving when he remembered them. Gratitude for their precious fellowship motivated *eucharisteo or* thanksgiving. Both gratitude and thanksgiving are derived from grace *charis* and characterize the grace-gathered community. Complaining creates toxic environments, stifles worship, and misdirects the focus of service. A grateful congregation is a grace-filled congregation and a healthy environment for growth.

Perhaps his memory turned to the prayer meeting at the port of Ephesus before he left them in parting tears. Where there is heartfelt gratitude, grace is close by. A healthy church is a prayerful congregation where the church shows care in word and deed.

Intercessory prayer is one way to express such care and love. The praying church is powerful. At its inception of the church on Pentecost, when the gathering prays, the life of Christ lives out in the unity of being empowered by the Spirit. Only eternity will reveal the full impact of a unified praying church where people minister to one another in love.

Grace-gathered people in Ephesus would be appealing and attractive to curious onlookers. The *ethos* of genuine commitment to Christ, loving one another, and prayer characterized the faithful people of the Lord. A gathering like this is unique in any culture. It just stands out in its sincerity, purity, and loving unity. A commitment to church health is a worthy goal of any Christian congregation. It should be cultivated and protected amid an uncaring and complacent world.

Grace and Knowledge

Grace and knowledge are the *ethos* of healthy congregations that focus on Christian discipleship. Jesus is the central focus of life, worship, faith, and practice. Spiritual growth does not happen apart from fellowship with Christ through the clear teaching of Scripture. A growing relationship with Christ embraces the believer's calling and rests in their future inheritance. Paul then prays specifically for such growth.

> That the God of our Lord Jesus Christ, the Father of glory, may give unto you the spirit of wisdom and revelation in the *knowledge* of him: The eyes of your understanding being enlightened; that you may *know* what the hope of his calling is, and what the riches of the glory of his inheritance in the saints,
> (Ephesians 1.15-17, KJBT)

Paul gives us an idea of how to pray for an unshakable and firm faith. Much like a mathematics teacher who desires that the students learn the elementary knowledge *gnosis* of math, Paul wants the believer to grow in an experiential knowledge of Jesus. The foundational precepts form the groundwork for more complex concepts.

As the student progresses through understanding the more "nuanced" knowledge *epignosis,* this eventually leads to fuller perception and application. The engineer's specialized knowledge works out in field application. Applying complex formulas rests firmly upon an understanding of the basic concepts.

Understanding the nature of God, our identity in Christ, and the power of the Holy Spirit's indwelling form the basic theological concepts for a growing community of faith. Doctrines exposited clearly from the context of Scripture had massive practical implications for the Ephesians. In a world that focuses on what is expedient or momentary pleasure, the followers of Christ live for the eternal.

Eternity shapes their thinking. The believer has a most excellent, confident expectation concerning the future. Abundantly rich beyond measure is the believer's standing. A glorious inheritance awaits the faithful called in Christ. What great assurances! Personal growth in knowing the Lord encourages deeper faith and greater confidence. Feelings of personal inadequacy fade when our faith rests firmly in Scripture. It is more than good feelings but personal faith grounded in Christ.

Wisdom & Illumination

> *That the God of our Lord Jesus Christ, the Father of glory, may give to you the spirit of wisdom and revelation in the knowledge of Him,* (Ephesians 1.17, KJBT)

As mentioned in the previous chapter, God the Father is personal and relational. Likewise, Jesus is also personable and relational, along with the person and work of the Holy Spirit. Being in Christ means we have the fullness of the Godhead, both intimately and personally. Paul's prayer is that the Holy Spirit leads them deeper into the wisdom of God's plan of salvation. A treasure trove of accessible knowledge is in Christ. (cf. Colossians 2.3)

Wisdom is the ability to apply what one knows as truth. Seeing Christ operating in our lives means that His life is being lived out for the glory of God, regardless of the circumstance.

God had delivered many Ephesians from the spiritual darkness of magic and cultic oracles. He illuminated the heart with the internal guidance of spiritual wisdom. The believer is empowered to follow the promptings and leadership of the Holy Spirit.

Revelation means uncovering or making known something not previously known. Believers knew that the Gospel of Christ only "scratched the surface" in understanding their relationship with God. Paul explores the rich depth of salvation, the beauty of Christ, and His work in salvation. He desired that they become settled into this glorious mystery and a firm assurance in Christ.

Christian parents desire their children's faith to be both serious and settled. Parents hope their children's convictions run deep in Christ and not in this world that has run "off the rails" from reason and morality. Temptations are withstood only with a firm footing on biblical convictions.

Spiritual Insight

> *The eyes of your understanding are enlightened; that ye may know what the hope of his calling is, and what the*

> riches of the glory of his inheritance in the saints,
> (Ephesians 1.18, KJBT)

Paul uses a unique phrase (eyes of the soul) --used only here in the New Testament. He desires that the believer have insightful, spiritual perception. Discernment is closely associated with this concept. The believer needs insight into situations, issues, beliefs, and life.

Paul wants them to discern life (what they saw and heard in culture) through the nature of God. Think of a student sitting in one of the esteemed lecture halls in Ephesus. Hearing the learned philosophers of their day, how might a student understand what they are hearing from their Christian worldview? Evaluating and examining the worldview behind what they are hearing would be essential. What about a Christian young person navigating a culture of moral degradation? How important is spiritual insight? How would such a faith inform business transactions in the marketplace?

Navigating the cultural *ethos* and influences requires wisdom, illumination, and keen spiritual perception. Our thinking needs input outside our limited thoughts, perceptions, and feelings. And we need wisdom, direction, and input greater than our experiences. What we need is truth from God's perspective. God's Word conforms to His Holy nature in all righteousness and goodness. It is the truth of His will and purpose bearing upon our minds and hearts.

A mind anchored in the reality of truth and a conscience informed by Scripture is crucial where moral confusion prevails. Spiritual insight is needed today more than ever. Declaring the gospel and expositing the Scripture is the church's mission. Clarity is essential to this task.

An atmosphere of encouragement helps faith grow into faithfulness to Christ. Facing a barrage of worldviews and massive cultural confusion, believers should pray for one another. Pray for a dedicated, purposeful life that values the eternal and glorious riches of Christ. Live with a greater purpose than the temporary fads the world offers.

Pray for self-mastery of emotions and passions surrendered to Christ and firmly planted in truth. In a world given to nihilism, the human heart still longs for hope. Pray our hope is in Christ alone. Pray for a confident expectation in Christ that yields a deep and satisfying joy.

Hope for their Calling

The *ethos* of a healthy church always operates in hope. Hope is the essence of Christian service and ministry. Hope is the firm, confident expectation of good. This idea of good stems from the nature of God's goodness at work. God does good because He is good. It is the expectation of future good in Christ and especially in His complete rescue.

Remember the previous verses 4-14, Paul outlines the magnitude of spiritual blessings. He is praying that these truths become the bedrock of how they view God, themselves, and one another. There is reason for confidence in their calling in the gospel. It is the foundation for a deeper life of faith. It is their very future hope and the completion of their calling in Christ. Paul prays that believers become thoroughly convinced of what they have in their standing in Christ.

An Inheritance of the Lord

In earlier verses, Paul describes the believers as chosen, adopted, and called saints. The Holy Spirit secures a glorious future inheritance in Christ. But there is more to this idea of inheritance. Believers are God's inheritance in the world. Believers are God's purchased possession. He entrusts us as being His inheritance.

The believer bears the name of his Heavenly Father. In Hebrew culture, children were considered a heritage of the Lord. (Psalm 127.3) Like a proud parent, our Heavenly Father claims us as His own. God's children are not a nuisance but a display of His image. God takes the broken pieces and claims believers as His children.

As the Psalmist declares, He *brought me out into a broad place; he rescued me because he delighted in me (Psalm 18.19, ESV).*

Pray that this truth sinks deeply into every aspect of our life. God delights in His children like a loving Father!

His Great Power Toward Us

The church's uniqueness is that the life of God operates in it. The *ethos* of the grace-gathered church is that it is divinely empowered. It is humbling to think that nothing of eternal significance happens apart from the work of the Holy Spirit.

Paul seemingly piles on adjectives that display the vastness of God's power at work within believers.

> What *is* the exceeding greatness of His power toward us who believe, according to the working of His mighty power. (Ephesians 1.19, KJBT)

Take notice of the numerous words that describe this operative power. God's power is dynamic and operative. This power exceeds any usual mark and beyond a vast magnitude. It is a "mega" power. His power is greater and more expansive than anything your mind imagines or encounters. Christ pervades and operates in every imaginable facet of life.

Think of the context of Ephesus, that widely held belief in magic, the demonic, and the power of the gods. These powers pale in comparison to the magnitude of God's power. His power is the ability and energy to perform and accomplish His will. Paul hits every angle of omnipotence, so the church recognizes God's power is all-pervasive!

Remember that Paul wants believers to realize that all they have in Christ is all they need. Christ is far above anything in heaven or earth. Feelings of weakness, inadequacy, or inability are no match to the mighty empowerment of the Spirit's indwelling. The power indwelling you is greater than the pressures surrounding you! God can do more than we ask or think! (cf. Ephesians 3.20)

Christ's Ruling Authority

Christ not only empowers the believer in the present moment, but He rules the future. The church keeps her focus on Christ in worship, ministry, fellowship, and prayer. It is our forward-looking ethos. We look to Jesus, the author and finisher of our faith.

Anticipating any uncertainty in the future can bring fear to the heart. The imagination can run wild, holding our emotions in the stronghold of fear. Jesus is on the throne and seated as the final authority *exousia* over everything, including the future and how we feel about it. Resting in the Lordship of Christ brings tranquility to the anxious soul. When our mind, stays upon Christ, then peace is interwoven in the day.

The indwelling power of the Holy Spirit is the same power that raised Jesus from the dead and seated Him in a place of authority. Authority here is again another aspect of the deposition of His power. Jesus' work is not only operative and dynamic, but He remains in the "seated appointment" ruling at the right hand of God.

> Which he worked in Christ, when he raised him from the dead, and set him at his own right hand in the heavenly places, Far above all principality, and power, and might, and dominion, and every name that is named, not only in this world but also in that which is to come:
> (Ephesians 1.20, KJBT)

Christ's authoritative position is His preeminence over and surpasses any power of principalities, *arche* and magisterial ruling authority in heavenly realms, over demonic influences and rulers of spiritual dominions.

As there is reality in the physical realm, there is also the reality of an unseen spiritual realm. It is just as real as the physical reality. Paul concludes that anything named, anyone possessing a title of honor, or anything in the future is under Christ's authority. Jesus is over it all, completely, and finally!

Many in the larger religious environment of Ephesus would capitalize on fear and encourage the purchase of magic to free them from the spirits in the unseen reality. Paul wants the Ephesian believers to rest in the Captain of their Salvation. Seated at the right hand of the Heavenly Father, He fights the earthly battles of the soul.

Christ wields the sword of the Spirit through the Word of God. All things in heaven and earth are under His sovereign authority. This truth clears the fog of confusion and relieves unnecessary fear. It provides the bedrock for personal belief in Christ that solidifies personal conviction. He is trustworthy with your future!

Christ's Consuming Authority

If Paul were here today, he would want 21st-century believers to know Jesus and grow in the knowledge of Him. Jesus was more than a religious figure who impacted cultures, leaving an indelible mark on the pages of human history. He is the Coming King at the consummation of time.

> And has put all things under his feet and made him the head over all things to the church which is his body, the fullness of him who fills all in all.
> (Ephesians 1.22-23, KJBT)

Jesus' teaching was a superior ethical understanding and religious instruction. His teaching was unlike the religious authorities of His day. Yet, He was more than a teacher. Jesus was a healer who made demons tremble. He expelled their domination and influence. Jesus restored dead bodies and cured physical maladies. Yet, He was more than the provider of salvation. Jesus was Immanuel-God with us. He is the God over all things at all times!

The church celebrates Christ's victory: past, present, and future. In Jesus' reign, He puts all things under His feet. Hearkening to the messianic overtones of Psalm 110. It is known as a royal enthronement Psalm as noted by scholars:

> The Lord said to my Lord, "Sit at My right hand, Till I make Your enemies Your footstool. The Lord shall send the rod of Your strength out of Zion rule in the midst of Your enemies.
> (Psalm 110.1-2, NKJV)

In Jesus' regal authority, He rules as head over the church in the present age. The grace-gathering community represents the kingdom of light in a broken, spiritually darkened world. Jesus so loved the church that He gave himself for her. His spotless bride, without blemish, will be presented to the heavenly Father and the heavenly hosts. (cf. Ephesians 5.27). What a glorious plan He has for us!

The church is God's only plan in this chaotic world. He is the head of the body. He is the Lord who rules in and through His body. The church is the very life of Christ in this world.

In the words of Paul to the Colossian believers:

> For God in all his fullness was pleased to live in Christ, and through him God reconciled everything to himself. He is the exalted Christ, whom every knee will bow down and acknowledge as Lord.
> (Colossians 1:19-20, NLT)

Jesus is the head of the gathering of His people. Believers have their all-sufficient standing in Christ's strength and empowerment through His Spirit. The believer is fully complete in Him. The Christian life then is Christ plus nothing. Christ has power over all things, whether in heaven, earth, seen and unseen. He is bringing everything unto Himself, including His people, who will appear with Him in glory for the glory of God the Father.

Conclusion

Spiritual growth is the fruit of a healthy church. Personal growth involves believers understanding their identity in Christ and the Holy Spirit's indwelling and power. Growing in the knowledge of the Lord is growing in grace. Such a healthy congregation then focuses upon Christ in worship, fellowship, teaching, ministry, and evangelism.

Paul prays for the believer's spiritual illumination, perception, insight, and wisdom. Realizing our inheritance in the Lord is essential to spiritual growth. Our Heavenly Father desires that we fully know Him until the day we see Him face to face. He is committed to our spiritual growth and a healthy *ethos* in His grace gathering.

I pray that your faith is grounded in the firm conviction that Jesus is the "one and only" way. Jesus is the life of the church and each of us! He is our very source and essence! The church is God's chosen means to put Jesus on grand display in the world! That others may view the beauty of His salvation and stand amazed. A broken world needs the hope that the fragmented pieces of their life can become their testimony of the wholeness experienced in Christ. Remember you are a living testimony of how Jesus forgives and restores! So, lift Him up highly!

A Masterpiece in the Making

Chapter Four

Ephesians 2.1-10

My sophomore high school picture was a disaster. Once I got the pictures, I hid them. I felt so ashamed. The look was not what I hoped for or imagined, and now undeniably in print. I hid the pictures out-of-sight of my mom behind the previous year's picture. She eventually found them!

She warned me that the permanent might not take very well with my finely textured hair. Throwing caution to the wind, I went for it anyway! The curly I wanted turned out to be an electrified frizz. I detested it.

With my failed hair project went my angle for acceptance and belonging among my peers. It opened my eyes to understand myself better. My aspirations and trust landed on temporary things rather than eternal pursuits. It's subtle, but it happens.

Since man's disobedience in the garden, man's internal compass is toward pleasing himself rather than God. Our direction and motivation are self-centered. We tend to shape our lives by what is around us rather than God's will for us. That image conforms to the world around us and our flesh. God has a new identity for us that corresponds to the reality of how he created us as human beings. It is always more satisfying than our self-made efforts.

Embracing our identity in Christ enables us to break free from destructive thinking and habits. We can live confidently in His will. We can be all that God intends us to be. The spiritual blessing in Christ is the new identity of individuals in the grace community.

This Scripture section summarizes the "before picture" alienated from a relationship with Christ and the "after picture" being in Christ. The "in Christ" picture is being human as God originally intended!

A Dreadful "Before" Picture

Many people desire a limitless life without boundaries and full of adventure. Such a life is unrealistic. It would be like a basketball game without boundary lines and the game rules in constant flux. It would make a chaotic and miserable game.

A culture of moral ambiguity seeks freedom without order and finds bondage instead. Any sense of personal satisfaction gets lost in the process. Our happiness is directly proportional to holiness. Our condition before Christ was a living spiritual death in the bondage of sin, dead in its trespasses. It was dreadful.

> And he has made you alive, who were dead in trespasses and sins. In time past you walked according to the course of this world, according to the prince of the power of the air, the spirit that now works in the children of disobedience: Among whom we also had Our way of living in times past in the lusts of our flesh, fulfilling the desires of the flesh and of the mind; and were by nature the children of wrath even as others.
> (Ephesians 2.1-3, KJBT)

A Dreadful Past

Before and after pictures are always revealing and often motivate us. Perhaps this is Paul's before and after picture. Recalling his spiritual condition before meeting Christ on the Road to Damascus, Paul was deeply grateful for saving grace. Gratitude is a much purer motivation for Christian living than guilt or shame, and love for Christ is the purest motivation. So, just how bad was the before picture? Let us look at the word picture.

Paul describes the characteristics of this spiritual death. It was our "mode of operation" being lived solely on the level of our senses: sight, touch, feel, smell, hearing. Being driven by their sinful nature, man is futile in thinking, and motivation is self-oriented, by nature trespassing against God's righteous demands.

Spiritual Death

Being spiritually dead to God, the inward working of the soul was informed, motivated, and operated only by the flesh—acting in rebellion as enemies of God. Sinful men can perform good deeds. However, he is unable to bridge the chasm between himself and God. Man is unable to save himself. Radio teacher Charles Swindoll summed it up well, "We were not as bad as we could be, but we were as bad off as we could be" without Christ. Paul's epistle to the Romans unpacks all of this more fully.

Genesis 3 provides the context for understanding spiritual death. As instructed by their Creator that the fruit of the "Tree of Knowledge of Good and Evil" was forbidden, they had the choice of either loving obedience and life or disobedience and death. In their deception and consequent trespass, they forfeited their relationship and fellowship with God. This act of rebellion severed any spiritual vitality. This spiritual death would eventually lead to their return to the dust.

It was a dreadful fall from moral and spiritual uprightness. There was an immediate spiritual death in their relationship with God. Through inherent guilt, they shamefully hide themselves in the depths of the garden. Neither their guilt nor spiritual death was something that fig leaves could cover or running from God could fix.

Spiritual death was only the beginning of the death curse. Their soul (mind, emotion , and will) would be in a progressive death that would affect all human relationships. Broken hearts and broken relationships are all ruined by sinful acts derived from an internal bent toward rebellion against the Creator. The reality of humanity's sinfulness explains the unwelcome news we get on our news feeds. Physical death (separation of the physical body and soul) would eventually follow.

Destructive Direction

Being destitute of the life of God means that we are powerless to break free from sin. The direction and progression of our personal lives are no different than the observable ways of the destruction of the world. It is a well-worn road ultimately motivated by the devil, who is in direct rebellion against God.

This present darkness is under the domain of "the prince of the power of the air"–Satan. The original rebel diabolically influences, persuades, manipulates, and controls the rebellion. He is under the wrath of the Creator and will face judgment. Satan is the menace behind man's rebellious nature. Paul describes this as the spirit at work in the children of disobedience being obstinate and in opposition to God.

How do such rebels live? They did not have to look far; Ephesus was a Gentile city given over to gratifying the sinful nature. Gentiles were known for living unbridled in the inordinate desires of the flesh. The economy and religion of Greek society in Ephesus were predominately sensual and violated the moral sensibilities of Jews and Christians. Ephesus was the best the world *cosmos* system could offer. The arrangements and ornaments centered around the lust of the eye, the flesh, and the pride of life.

Being given over to sin, in their thinking and lifestyle, they became corrupt in all their ways. All idolatry, evil, sin, and corruption are on a collision course with God, who brings every thought, deed, and action in the light of His righteous judgment. Paul describes the worst imaginable "before picture." Man is pictured bound in the shackles of sin, completely missing the mark of God's glory. The dregs of guilt and shame await the cup of His wrath.

The prince and power of the air will be judged, along with those following the way of rebellion. Humanity was without Christ and hope and on a collision course with the God who created him in His image. The outcome is devastating without God's gracious inter- vention. Thank God, mercy reached down, making alive those in Christ.

Made Alive Together

As much as the dreadfulness of the before picture, the hope-filled phrase "but God" changed the trajectory of human history. God chooses to intervene with mercy in the grace gift freely given by God and received by faith. This grace cannot be earned or bought. God's mercy is the withholding of deserved judgment, while grace is God pouring out His favored kindness. Take particular note of the wording in this verse. Believers are being made alive, raised, and seated together with Christ. Christian growth does not happen in isolation. It happens together!

> But God, who is rich in mercy, for His great love with which He loved us, even when we were dead in trespasses, made us alive together with Christ (by grace you have been saved), and raised *us* up together, and made *us* sit together in the heavenly *places* in Christ Jesus: (Ephesians 2.3-4, KJBT)

As noted in previous chapters, being "in Christ" forms a significant theological understanding of the believer's new position. Paul shifts the epistles' emphasis from being "in Christ" to being "with Christ" now. Believers have more than a new standing but "presence" together. Christ presents believers as a marvelous display of God's mercy and grace. He shows forth the richness of God's mercy before the heavenly hosts.

The believer has a new identity "in Christ" and a co-identification "with Christ" in His death, burial, and resurrection.

> That in the ages to come he might show the exceeding riches of his grace in *his* kindness toward us through Christ Jesus. For by grace, you are saved through faith; and that not of yourselves; *it is* the gift of God, not of works, lest anyone should boast.
> (Ephesians 2.5-9, KJBT)

God's gracious kindness will be on display for all of eternity. It is God's goodness in action. It is the good God who desires His children to experience His goodness. A. W. Tozer describes this in The *Knowledge of the Holy* as the inclination of God through His nature to "bestow blessedness" and take "holy pleasure in the happiness of His people."[1] The doctrine of salvation is clear. The believer's salvation is from God's loving intention. The grace gift extends from His goodness to all who receive by faith.

---

[1] A.W. Tozer, The Knowledge of the Holy, Harper Collins Publication, New York, 1961, 16.

So, salvation is not self-derived, earned, acquired, or obtained through human sincerity, performance, or merit. Grace is not what you are working for, but grace is what is working for you in Christ. Therefore, biblical Christianity is unique among world religions. Human effort and self-derived righteousness are the basis of all world religions. The Bible teaches that God reaches for humanity in Christ through the gospel of grace. Human effort cannot purchase a gift. Grace is Christ's work on your behalf, putting you in the right relationship with God. Grace is amazing!

God's Masterpiece

Much like a symphony performing a beautiful piece of choral music, a poetic presentation of stirring prose, or an artistic sculpture, the work of creative artists is inspiring. The creator of a poem uses imagination, skill, and abilities in structuring the right words, voice, tone, and inflection for effect. The poem is the poet's creation. It is "made" by his doing. The work is a reflection of the creator.

> For we are his workmanship, created in Christ Jesus unto good works, which God has before ordained that we should walk in them. (Ephesians 2.10, KJBT)

His Workmanship

The believer is God's masterpiece on display! *Poima* is translated handiwork or masterpiece in the New Living Translation. The grace-gathering is like a poem displaying the depth of God's loving- kindness. As God's masterpieces, we are living examples of the handiwork of the Heavenly Father.

God sings the song of redemptive love over us for all to hear. As we are His workmanship, we are on display as a new creation. The redeemed from the fall are God's purchased possessions, being conformed to the image of Christ. They reflect His glory and the richness of His grace. Let us explore a bit more.

In the garden paradise, the creation of man was perfect–in the likeness of God. What does this mean? God is Spirit without the imposition of physical limitations. Adam and Eve were created as both rational and relational creatures. Man thinks and relates to others on a personal level. In other words, man has a moral constitution.[2]

Humanity possesses an innate sense of right and wrong. Morality runs deeper than learned behaviors but is inherent in being human. Man's conscience, however operative, is condemned because of the inward awareness that there is a God. Therefore, because of this knowledge of God, all humanity is without excuse before Him.

God's breath of life filled the lifeless form of Adam, and he became a living soul. The curse of death followed their rebellious fall. Their physical lives became devoid of spiritual life and a certain eternal death awaiting. Man is in an irreconcilable place unless God graciously intervenes.

A New Creation in Christ

In Christ, a "new creation" arises, breaking free from the stronghold of sin and death. Therefore, if anyone *is* in Christ, *he is* a new creation; old things have passed away; behold, all things have become new. (cf. 1 Corinthians 5.17) It is a new kind of life in Christ. It is a vibrant, living relationship and fellowship with the Heavenly Father. The old life is behind you, and the past sinful lifestyles, habits, guilt, and condemnation are just that--the past. So, Jesus replaces your spiritual death with a new life and a marvelous future. You will share in His glory. Until the time of your ultimate glorification with Him, He places you in a new community of grace–a grace gathering where you can grow in His likeness.

Good Works

The kingdoms of this world display divisions and differences. Identified by social class and belief systems, people get stuck with demographic group labels and ideologies. Because there are causes "aplenty" to align with today, many people feel there is good reason to be divisive. The kingdom message of the Gospel is greater than any earthly cause. The church breaks through these divisions with a gospel

---

[2] Leroy Forlines, The Quest for Truth: Answering Life Inescapable Questions, Randall House, Nashville, 2001. 139...Forlines discussion on the moral and functional likeness of human make-up is very helpful for extended study and consideration.

for everyone, no matter race, ethnicity, background, or status. All who come into God's kingdom are self-professed rebels against God, turning from rebellion to repentance by humbly receiving God's offer of salvation and identity in Christ.

Such was the Ephesian church. Divided by ethnicity, religion, and such before Christ, now there is a new gathering of redeemed people. Animosity ceases, and the fissures of division can heal in this new community. The world has a hard time believing that such love exists, or such a community can thrive, but it does in Christ. The kingdom of light brought together Jews–God's chosen covenant people; and Gentiles–those outside the covenant. They were one gathering in Christ. So, the church is a uniquely gathered community in a world of division.

This gathering has the purpose of good works in Christ. It has a pertinent message for all nations. The church from every nation, tongue, tribe, and ethnicity is one in Christ. It is a rich, life-changing gospel for everyone, everywhere and at all times. It is truly miraculous. In a world that divides up to gain earthly power, Christ makes a unified body as one. He takes those broken by sin and the world system and molds a masterpiece.

Centered upon the person of Christ, the church's message is good news in a broken world. That good news calls for repentance of sin and trust in God's provision through Christ. The church is His kingdom plan and given the ministry of reconciliation.

> Now all things *are* of God, who has reconciled us to Himself through Jesus Christ, and has given us the ministry of reconciliation. (2 Corinthians 5.18, NKJV)

Satan, the original rebel against God, drives a divided world system. The "Prince and power of the air" masquerades as an angel of light, deceiving people and diabolically influencing people in the rebellion. His purpose is to kill, steal, and destroy. He sows discontentment and discord in the church and draws our focus from Christ to ourselves and others. The course of the world follows his cues, and sometimes even our focus is drawn away from Christ.

Believers are ministers of reconciliation in this broken world. The healing balm is the gospel of Christ. Do not be surprised or dismayed if the world rejects the church and disparages her message of repentance. Souls in darkness prefer to remain in the darkness of personal destruction, division, and bondage. Yet, I am always amazed at how God breaks through the dark. He draws people to the light of personal restoration through the gospel. No matter a person's background or sin, God brings freedom and breaks bondage. It is a testimony of how God works in changing lives!

Prepared Works

The works of God are pre-prepared. These works are purposeful and unfold from divine counsel. You were not born out of season, and you are not born again without reason. You are "in Christ" for such a time as this. Jesus promised His disciples that they would do even greater works. They often messed up, felt uncertain and inadequate, and fell short of God's glory, but God used them mightily. God created them with a purpose to fulfill.

God is not waiting on perfect people or a perfect church; He will make her perfect one day. God powerfully uses a grace-filled body carrying the gospel in a broken world, showing the world the works of God. You are displaying the gracious Christ as His ambassador of grace and truth!

You have a spiritual authority to walk in. Remember, Jesus told His disciples before He sent them out as His servants to minister to a wayward world.

> Behold, I give you the authority to trample on serpents and scorpions, and over all the power of the enemy, and nothing shall by any means hurt you. (Luke 10.19, NKJV)

Tread on the serpents that continually strike at your feet. You have steps of victory to walk in. Your victory is Christ, and the world is watching. God is on display, and you are spiritually equipped for this time for the journey.

Conclusion

The redeemed are God's masterpieces of grace on glorious display in the heavenly realm. Angels marvel at God's workmanship. God brings us together and back to himself as one body. Sinners rescued! A dreadful past is forgiven and forgotten by God. The bondage is breaking. The future is certain! God's mercy and kindness extended in a clarion gospel call.

Walk in victory today. It does not appear what you will be, but when you see Jesus face to face, you will be in His perfect likeness. It will be better than any picture taken of you!

Jesus Keep Me Near the Cross
Fanny Crosby
1869—Public Domain

**Jesus, keep me near the cross,
There a precious fountain—
Free to all, a healing stream—
Flows from Calvary's mountain.
In the Cross, in the Cross
Be my glory ever
Till my raptured soul
shall find
Rest beyond the river.**

The Cross-Formed Community

Chapter Five

Ephesians 2.11-22

Moral ambiguity deepens today! A sense of alienation, isolation, loneliness, and a pervasive spiritual darkness envelops the culture. Riddled with anxiety, many lack internal calm or peace. Others feel a pervasive loneliness and emptiness. The subsequent brokenness within individuals expands the world.

Marked by conflict and division, the best the world offers breaks down. Societal stressors prevail due to human wickedness. Racism, crime, violence, and all social issues expose the conflict. Social issues are complex, and the problems are more than what meets the eye.

All these conditions are merely surface. It is just the tip of the iceberg–revealing the depth of human depravity and spiritual brokenness. Underneath lies a massive layer of spiritual alienation fueled by a sinful nature in rebellion with the Creator. Many disturbing cultural issues reflect the spiritual condition of the human heart.

As mentioned in a previous chapter, I take a yearly retreat to a monastery with fellow ministers. Our trip usually involves a casual and quiet stroll through the garden cemetery. Walking among the graves of these monks is sobering. This cemetery dates back to the monasteries' founding in 1848. The simple cross is planted firmly like the headstone over their graves. I wrote about this experience in *The Retreat of the Soul*, "The cross stands firmly planted in the earth, just like an exclamation point at the end of a sentence." The cross quietly shouts-- "The work is finished."[1]

---

[1] Sergent, Gregory H., Wells, James Eds., The Retreat of the Soul: Hopeway Books, Gate City, 2017, 85.

The message of the cross speaks directly to the heart broken by sin. God has commissioned the church's message. It is both pertinent and relevant. Forgiveness, wholeness, healing, and peace compel the rebel heart to the foot of the cross of Christ. As someone once said, there is equal footing at the cross because we're all broken. The cross was the instrument of Christ's brokenness, and His brokenness is the source of our wholeness. What a paradox! As a minister, I often have the congregation hear the wafer break as we remember Christ's broken body in communion.

The church is a cross-formed community of disciples following the steps of the Savior. Spiritual transformation begins at the cross and continues daily through being conformed to the cross of Christ.

The Cross

In the first century, the cross represented the cruelest form of tortuous execution. These events displayed the raw power of Rome and its commitment to extinguish rebellion in any form and preserve peace and social order. It motivated fearful compliance.

An emblem of intense suffering and pain, the cross was associated with rejection and shame. Interestingly, Jesus chose this imagery as His message in calling His disciples. The cross He preached would become His destiny by the will of the Father. Jesus called His disciples to "take up your cross and follow me."

Amazingly, they left everything and followed Him. Following this peripatetic rabbi in His school would involve self-denial, self-sacrifice, shame, and rejection. They gave all to follow Christ, and they did until they faced the grim reality of his execution; so, they mostly fled, and Peter even denied he knew him as the passion week turned bad on Good Friday. As they were in denial of the cross, Jesus was becoming obedient unto death, even the cross.

The gruesome scene of the cross left them disillusioned and dismayed. They could not have imagined the cross they picked would end in Jesus' death by crucifixion. The end of a Roman cross usually led the victims' carcass to the trash heap, left for vultures and wild animals.

They buried Jesus in a donated tomb. The disciples rehearsed every moment, including their disappointment and failure. But everything changed with the resurrection. The resurrection of Jesus changes everything. It always does!

These eyewitnesses became living witnesses to the world of new life in Christ. These disciples returned from the empty tomb to see the cross of Jesus in a whole new light. Jesus' words, "See here my hands and feet," are echoed through the gospel message. The hold of death is defeated, and His resurrected life means hope.

Jesus was not a martyr. He was the suffering Savior, spoken of in Isaiah 53. The chastisement of our peace was upon Him, and by His stripes is healing for the broken. The cross of Jesus was the message of the good news given to us in the Gospels.

Therefore, the history of the cross is not a refined symbol that adorns our churches. Repentant sinners cherish the cross of Jesus. Why? Jesus was our substitute. We deserve God's judgment for our rebellion. Jesus pays our penalty and offers forgiveness.

Herein lies the beauty and glory that compelled the songwriter's words, "So I'll cherish the old rugged cross…I will cling to the old rugged cross." It is a new life for the self-professed sinner who kneels at Jesus' feet. Life and peace happen at the cross. It is the foundation of Christian discipleship and the basis for a cross-formed community.

A Cross-Formed Community

What does it mean to become a cross-formed community? Paul gives the power of the cross for the Christian life.

> I am crucified with Christ, nevertheless, I live yet not I,
> it is Christ who lives in me, and the life I now live I live
> by faith in the Son of God.   (Galatians 2.20, NKJV)

It is a Christian disciple co-identified with Christ's death, burial, and resurrection. Christ's new life is empowering. The resurrected Lord lives among His grace-gathered people. So, the cross-formed community is a Christ-conformed community. So, let us unpack the community aspect of the grace gathering.

Brought Together

The Roman Empire was a conglomeration of people groups. Theirs was a history of being conquered through military expansion. Rome instituted the *Pax Romana* or the Roman Peace. Rome's massive military presence and roadways dissuaded rebellion against the empire. Emperor worship was one means of gaining allegiance to Rome and the state's attempt at unity among the provinces. It was a superficial peace at best and did not address racism and classism between the Greeks, barbarians, or the Jewish populace.

What Rome could offer would never resolve the issues of the heart. Manufactured solutions cannot fix spiritual problems. These verses give us insight into the social dynamic in Ephesus.

> Therefore remember that you, being in times past Gentiles in the flesh—who are called uncircumcision by what is called the circumcision made in the flesh by hands— that at that time you were without Christ, being aliens from the commonwealth of Israel and strangers from the covenants of promise, having no hope and without God in the world. But now in Christ Jesus you who once were far off have been brought near by the blood of Christ. (Ephesians 2. 11-13, KJBT)

Gentiles understood and felt the sense of separation and alienation in temple worship. The Gentiles were considered ceremonially impure. They were considered unclean as foreigners. They were socially isolated and shut out of access to fellowship with God. Being stationed in the outer court along with the money changers, the Gentiles were forbidden to enter the inner court. Written on stone inscriptions in Greek and Latin were posted as dire warnings to Gentiles who might wander and trespass the inner court. Death awaited transgressors.

The Gentiles were not part of the Abraham covenant. The sign of the covenant was circumcision. Being uncircumcised, they were considered pagan and heathen. Without the knowledge of God, they were shut out from relationship and intimacy with God and far from Him.

Paul describes the Gentile's dire situation as "without God." They neither knew nor worshiped the true God. They were godless in the purest sense of the word–without hope. Paul calls the Ephesian believers to remember. They were to recollect and even rehearse the blessing of life accessed in Christ.

Being without hope is man's desperate plight unless God intervenes. Like verse four, "But God" introduces our greatest hope. Paul wants Gentiles and Jews in the congregation to understand that the cross changes their life for eternity, but it brings them together now. The all-sufficient work forms the community of faith together as one.

> But now you have been united with Christ Jesus. Once you were far away from God, but now you have been brought near to him through the blood of Christ. For Christ himself has brought peace to us. He united Jews and Gentiles into one people when, in his own body on the cross, he broke down the wall of hostility that separated us. (Ephesians 2.13-14, KJBT)

Vertical — Peace with God

The new covenant in Christ's blood brings believers who were once enemies of God into a covenant relationship. Communion is the celebration of that covenant. The Lord's sacrifice brings believers together–united as one. Now reconciled and at peace. Paul expands our understanding of the nature of this peace brought through the cross in Colossians.

> For it pleased *the Father that* in Him all the fullness should dwell, and by Him to reconcile all things to Himself, by Him, whether things on earth or things in heaven, having made peace through the blood of His cross. And you, who once were alienated and enemies in your mind by wicked works, yet now He has reconciled in the body of His flesh through death, to present you holy, and blameless, and above reproach in His sight. (Colossians 1.21-22)

The believer's harmony with God solely depends upon Christ. There is no other way or means for peace and a harmonious relationship with God. Jesus is the *Prince of Peace*. He is our peace with God. Paul describes man's separation from the Father as the middle wall of partition. The commandments reveal that man at heart is a lawbreaker. Christ makes peace for us through the cross as the perfect lawkeeper. There is a legal and forensic quality in this peace. The penalty of our sin is fully paid at the cross.

> For he is our peace, who has made both one, and has broken down the middle wall of partition between us; Having abolished in his flesh the enmity, even the law of commandments contained in ordinances; in order to make in himself from two one new man, so making peace; (Ephesians 2. 14-15 KJBT)

Peace of God

Peace with God is the believer's new life. The peace of God becomes a subjective reality as the believer yields to Christ's Lordship in life circumstances. Peace is that tranquil state of the soul resting in the assurance of Christ's Lordship. Jesus promised us peace, unlike anything in this world. (cf. John 14.27) It encourages great confidence in our relationship with God. We should not be troubled or afraid because the Lord of peace is with us.

All the attributes described of the Father are attributes of the Son and the Holy Spirit. No earthly circumstance or experience is outside the scope of His awareness. He gives His peace as we trust Christ with the distress of the heart. In Colossians, Paul encourages believers to "Let the peace of God rule." (cf. Colossians 3.15) God's peace will be the ruling umpire to guide us. The peace of Jesus has far-reaching implications to explore, especially in your personal experience.

Belonging Together

Salvation is a blessing for the individual who receives it through repentance and faith. The vertical crossbeam of God's perfect love brings us peace with God. It does not stop there. There is a horizontal crossbeam. Jesus' arms of love extend to everyone. Hostilities cease with God and in human relationships. Diverse ethnic communities become one in Christ as brothers and sisters. The Gospel of Christ accomplishes what Rome could not–a community of peace.

Repentant sinners from every nation, tongue, and tribe stand equal at the foot of the cross. No one is turned away from a relationship with Christ at the cross. All divisions crumble. The cross-formed community is a new community living in harmony and unity. It is both loving and peace-filled. The world takes notice!

Peace among Men

The believer is now in a harmonious relationship with the Father because of Christ's cross. Jews and Greeks live in the light and blessing of this kingdom. Part of that blessing is the hopeful greeting *shalom* is realized in Christ. In a world that plays up division and conflict, what a powerful testimony of the gospel that harmoniously brings together as one the body of Christ in peace.

> Paul describes this as the preaching of the gospel, And that he might reconcile both unto God in one body by the cross, having slain the enmity by it: And came and preached peace to you who were far off, and to those who were near. (Ephesians 3.15-16 KJBT)

Bringing unlikely people groups together is the work of the gospel.

Death is the great equalizer. It does not respect anything we hold as meritorious–status, money, prestige, or nationality. Death gets us all because we all are sinners. Sinners can meet Jesus at the cross and find new life and an empowering love.

Reconciled

We meet Jesus at the cross. His sacrifice is a bearing of the believer's shame, paying the penalty of sin. For those mystified by suffering, the Bible reveals that God the Son experienced the curse of sin and death for us. Just look at the cross. God the Son willingly experienced the most horrific suffering. He meets us with our questions and in our pain as our High Priest. What appeared to be an apparent injustice on the human level met the demands of divine justice. Jesus endured the cross and disregarded the shame.

> And that he might reconcile both unto God in one body by the cross, having slain the enmity by it: And came and

> preached peace to you who were far off, and to those who were near. For through him we both have access by one Spirit unto the Father. Now therefore you are no longer strangers and foreigners, but fellow citizens with the saints, and of the household of God;
> (Ephesians 2. 16-22, KJBT)

Reconciliation is the believer's harmony with God through the completed work of God. Sin breaks our fellowship. Confession of sin means an agreement with God about our sinful actions or omissions. Any failure that falls short of the glory of God is reconcilable. The new community lives as the reconciled people of God with the ministry of reconciliation in the world. The gospel simply changes hearts and changes the world for the better.

Made-Near

The term here reflects the Gentile proselyte brought into Judaism. They are now near. There were a series of courts and walls surrounding the Temple. The court of the priests, the court of the Israelites reserved for the ritually pure males, the court of the women, and the outer court of the Gentiles. The Gentiles were considered unclean and not allowed past the walled barriers without fear for their lives.

The separation was a barrier. It was intentional. The Gentiles were not privileged to the benefits of the temple. The cross of Jesus brings reconciliation with God, and now they are brought near to God as a new community. The dividing partition that separates people is now gone. Everyone has access to the Father.

Access

The believer now has access–a favorable approach to God. Because of the cross of Christ, the believer is granted admission before the unapproachable God through the Holy Spirit. Like an announcement of a subject to the king, the believer now has access to the most holy. The temple veil ripped from top to bottom during Christ's crucifixion. The inner sanctuary is now accessible to everyone. A historical happening remains a remarkable biblical symbol of the far-reaching mercy of God.

Paul reminds the Roman believers of this grand admission, "We have access by faith into this grace in which we stand and rejoice in the hope of the glory of God." (Romans 5.2) It is the undeserved gracious opportunity to behold the glory of God now and in the future.

> Through Him we also have access by faith into this [remarkable state of] grace in which we [firmly and safely and securely] stand. Let us rejoice in our hope *and* the confident assurance of [experiencing and enjoying] the glory of [our great] God [the manifestation of His excellence and power]. (Romans 5.2, AMP)

The Holy Spirit makes the body one and gives us access to the Father. We are no longer treated as strangers or without a way to the Father, but now the believer is made acceptable as friends of God. We take joy in the assurance that the Father is approachable and we can come boldly to the throne of grace. We are God's household, fellow citizens, and a spiritual household. Saints are holy and without blame.

Builds-Up Together

In the new building, Christ is the cornerstone that is the foundation of the teaching of the apostles. As a building, it is being constructed and built up through edification. Ultimately, the people of God are the consecrated habitation of His presence.

New Citizenship

Believers are now fellow citizens and have communion with the saints. Like Israel, who were heirs of the Abrahamic blessing, believers are heirs of God's promise. It is a grace gathering that forms the people of God, a royal priesthood, and a holy nation. The church is God's precious treasure called forth to His praise among the nations.

New Household

The household of God is standing upon a solid foundation. The Gospel of the Cross is the central message of the gathering, and Jesus Christ is the identity of the new community. Jesus is the center and foundation of the Christian life. The Apostle's message was thoroughly Christ-centered. The church gathers and grows together as a holy temple, being the habitation of God.

> And are built upon the foundation of the apostles and prophets, Jesus Christ himself being the chief cornerstone; In whom all the building rightly framed together grows unto a holy temple in the Lord: In whom you also are built together for a habitation of God through the Spirit. (Ephesians 2. 20-22, KJBT)

This beautiful imagery of Jesus being the cornerstone where all the other stones are aligned. The building of God is framed together and built up or constructed as holy to the Lord. As God's dwelling place and the church grows in the work of ministry.

New Temple

The church is the new temple, the habitation of God. The center of life for the twelve tribes was the Tabernacle. The tribes flanked every side of it. The presence of God (*shekinah-glory*) would fill the Holiest of Holies. The high priest would approach to make yearly atonement. In essence, the presence of God was literally at the center of all their life.

Jesus was the temple of the Holy Spirit, and now believers are the temple of the Holy Spirit, the habitation of God. Christ is the foundation and fills the temple with Himself. The grace-gathering is more than a social organization held together by mission, values, and goals. It is a dynamic, living entity in the world where Jesus lives.

The new temple bears the life of God through His spirit in a world in the throes of death and destruction. The church is light dispelling the darkness, salt that purifies and preserves. The message is one of healing and lasting hope. What a privilege to be part of a local grace gathering where Christ's life lives among His people.

Conclusion

The church's message says that God is up to something good in a world filled with chaos and confusion. The cross is the symbol that has shaped human history by transforming lives and becoming the catalyst for positive good in the larger culture. It is the underlying motivation of multitudes of missionary outreaches with the message of the cross. The cross is the church's central message. It is the message preached from her pulpit. It is the message of the Apostles and ours today!

Wherever there are the lost, the gospel penetrates. Wherever there is suffering, the cross-formed church goes to the rescue. It's the motivation of Christian relief organizations, the establishment of hospitals, orphanages, Bible distributions, and numerous missionary efforts. It is a believable message to be received. God brings broken people together in salvation and restoration.

The church is unique in that regard. The church stands at the threshold of hell and conquerors. Why? Her Savior has won the victory on the cross through the glorious resurrection. Christ will not fail.

The Gospel of Grace

Sola Christus
in Christ alone

Sola Gratia
by grace alone

Sola Fide
through faith alone

Sola Scriptura
in the authority of Scripture alone

Sola Deo Gloria
for the Glory of God alone

Getting the Gospel Right

Chapter Six

Ephesians 3.1-12

I cannot think of a more pressing need for the church today than clearly articulating the Gospel. Proclaiming the Gospel is the primary mission of the church in the world. Living the gospel in the world makes the message credible.

But what is the gospel? The term is loosely used and understood, I fear. The clarity of the gospel was a pressing issue for first-century believers; it remains so in our day. Why is it that important? How we answer that question is germane to eternity. The Apostles defined the gospel as Christ's death, burial, and resurrection of Christ. Jesus came in fulfillment of the Scriptures. Jesus is all-sufficient for the salvation of repenting sinners who place trust in Christ by faith.

One of the first issues addressed by the early church was, "Should a person first become Jewish and receive the sign of God's covenant people through circumcision?" The Jerusalem Council answered decisively "no" in Acts 15. Christ alone was sufficient for salvation. Paul constantly encountered Judaizers who attempted to subvert the gospel message with works and place legalistic restrictions upon people.

On the other hand, Paul also dealt with the influences of the larger Greek religious culture. Some tried to syncretize philosophy, traditional observances, or the worship of angels into the gospel message. Paul addressed this issue with Colossian believers and exalted the supremacy of Christ in his letter. Why? Because the clarity of the gospel centers on a correct understanding of the person and work of Christ. Paul addresses what a gospel-transformed life looks like in the latter chapters of Ephesians.

Toward the end of Paul's ministry, he warned Timothy that people would not endure sound doctrine in the last days. Peter the Apostle always warned that false teachers with "itching ears" would subvert the purity of the gospel to gain hearers. Some teachers would even make disciples unto themselves and lead people into gross immorality. Contending for the faith requires contending for a pure Gospel in a thoroughly Christ-centered community. Jude considered it a worthy pursuit.

Adding works to the gospel of grace makes it "another gospel." A grace community clearly articulates the gospel of grace through faith in Christ alone. Good works are the evidence of the life-changing gospel, not the cause. A diluted gospel through cultural filters becomes a message that diminishes or compromises on sin. Turning from sin and trusting Christ by faith is essential to the gospel message. Repentance is an agreement with God about sin, a godly sorrow for sin, and then willfully turning from sin.

Paul staunchly defended the sufficiency of Christ's death, burial, and resurrection of Christ. Man's eternal destiny rests on the truth of the person of Jesus Christ and the gospel message.

The Apostle Paul

Paul had the evangelistic desire of a missionary and a heart of care and concern as a pastor, and now a prisoner for the gospel that he preached. This Apostle to the Gentiles describes his responsibility and stewardship of this gospel ministry and the far-reaching extent of God's grace to them.

Within the larger religious environment of Ephesus that promoted a mystical, higher esoteric spiritual knowledge to know God, Paul reminds them that the real mystery of the gospel is Christ. A general outline unfolds in this chapter: (1) Paul's *Stewardship* of the Mystery of Grace Vss. 1-6 (2) Paul's *Ministry* in God's Grace. Vss. 7-11 (3) Paul's *Pastoral* Prayer for Believers. Vss. 12-21

Paul the Prisoner

Paul pulls back the veil of his troubling situation, being under house arrest in Rome for preaching the gospel to the Gentiles. He would have possessed certain liberties and received visits from people, but he would have been in the sight of a Roman soldier.

In the Roman Empire, authorities were suspicious of the Christian religion. It was legally unrecognized. From their standpoint, this new religious sect was mysterious, misunderstood, and eventually persecuted. Paul would have been a 'figurehead' of this group. His imprisonment might have curtailed Christian missionary activities. Paul did not want the believers in Ephesus to lose heart *ekkakeo* or become *exhausted and weary* at his tribulations, vs. 13. Paul was sensing the pressure and distress from his confinement.

As a steward of the gospel, Paul was an overseer, minister, and pastor from a distance. The only tool at his disposal was writing letters and faithful friends in ministry who would serve as carriers. He was overwhelmed with his responsibility and calling. His prayer was that his house arrest would strengthen their faith. It was for the Gentile's glory. His calling was a dispensation or stewardship in fulfilling God's plan through Him. How Paul handled such a difficult circumstance is indeed insightful!

First, he saw himself as a prisoner of the Lord and not a prisoner of Rome. He was not a victim of circumstance or the fate of the gods. Paul viewed his imprisonment as sifted through the hands of sovereignty. He was trusting it all to Christ's Lordship. Secondly, Paul focused on his calling and ministry. He was trusting in God and making the best of a difficult situation.

Toward the end of Paul's life, his suffering was more intense in a cold Roman jail. His conviction concerning the gospel was even more settled. He admonished young Timothy to "not be ashamed of the testimony of the Lord," but to share in the suffering for the gospel. (cf. 2 Timothy 1.8)

He considered himself a prisoner of Christ and the testimony of the Lord. His feet and hands held heavy shackles, but a heavier weight was the burden of this good news of Christ to the world that lay heavy upon his heart.

Paul the Overseer

Paul now describes his calling as a dispensation. He is like an overseer of a household or a property administrator. The glorious mystery of the gospel is for everyone.

> For this reason I Paul, the prisoner of Jesus Christ for you Gentiles, If you have heard of the dispensation of the grace of God which is given me toward you: How that by revelation he made known unto me the mystery; (as I wrote before in few words, By which, when you read, you may understand my knowledge in the mystery of Christ). (Ephesians 3. 1- 4, KJBT)

This gospel has been revealed (or laid bare), just like a light that shines into the darkness and exposes the reality of what was in the dark. The Gentiles were once alien and strangers to the commonwealth of Israel, but now they are made part of the kingdom. So, the truth of the gospel that first came to the Hebrews now includes the Gentiles.

The Foundation of the Gospel

The Gospel of Jesus Christ is the mystery revealed. Like Daniel's interpretation of the King's dream, Paul unveiled God's great kingdom plan that included the Gentiles. Daniel interpreted the King's dream of the rise and fall of three earthly kingdoms, then the rising of God's kingdom that will eclipse all worldly kingdoms. Here is a portion of Daniel's interpretation.

> "During the reigns of those kings, the God of heaven will set up a kingdom that will never be destroyed or conquered. It will crush all these kingdoms into nothingness, and it will stand forever.
> (Daniel 2.44, NKJV)

Like Daniel, Paul recognized that Jesus fulfilled the progressive revelation of the coming Messiah in the Old Testament. He sensed that the gospel to the Gentiles was integral to God's plan for all nations. He heartily referred to himself as the Apostle to the Gentile.

Illumination of the Person and Work of Christ

It is certainly possible that many of the Gentiles had never heard of Jesus Christ. Paul wanted the Ephesian believers to understand the person and work of Christ in salvation and the head of this new community. The mystery of God's councils is revealed through the Old Testament law, prophets, and national history and ultimately revealed in Christ.

Peter offered "a sure word of prophecy," while Paul understood the person of Jesus– the long-awaited Messiah, the perfect law keeper as the central person of the gospel. Christ's death on the cross was shameful and appears as a failure on a human level. From God's perspective, it was a victory over sin, suffering, and death. It was the message of the kingdom of God for all the world. This knowledge did not rest solely on his private revelations from God, but it was attested to by the Apostles and the Prophets by the Holy Spirit. Paul stirred up the urgency of the message confirmed in Scripture.

The All-Sufficient Work of Christ

Christ's all-sufficient and once-for-all work is unparalleled in its efficacy when compared to the religions of the world and their emphasis on human effort to appease God. Our works are simply inadequate when compared to Christ's cross. A self-derived righteousness or self-made morality cannot bridge the chasm between man and God. Christ's redemptive work on the cross is our only hope!

Early in church history, heretical teachers attempted to divest Jesus of His full humanity or divinity, diminishing the message of the cross. Understanding Christ's *hypostatic* union was later established in the Council of Chalcedon 451 AD. Understanding the sufficiency of Christ's work of salvation rests upon Jesus as the God-man. Without it, the gospel is not good news.

The 20th Century theological liberalism opted for a teacher Jesus with a superb ethical system, without the ideas of blood sacrifice and a cross. Others reinterpreted Jesus as a philosopher, prophet, or an enlightened mystic diverting attention away from the cross. Christ took our place on the cross. The writer of Hebrews speaks of the centrality of Christ's cross. He endured the cross, despised the shame, and now exalted at the right hand of God. (cf. Hebrews 12.2)

The central message of Jesus, the Apostles, the early church, and the church throughout human history pointed to the cross. The church uniquely preaches the gospel in evangelism, and the call to take up your cross is the message of discipleship for being conformed in the image of Christ.

Anglican Bishop J. C. Ryle, a 19th Century said, *A cheap Christianity without a cross will prove in the end to be a useless Christianity without a Crown.*

A crossless "Christianity" is a church without good news or hope. The world needs more than the social enterprise of the church. The cross saves people from an impending judgment. When people feel the weight of the gravity of sin, then the message of the cross is good news that it is.

Proclamation of Apostles & Prophets

Amazingly, we possess more than oral traditions. We have an accurate, recorded eyewitness account of Jesus's life and ministry. The Four Gospels (Matthew, Mark, Luke & John) form a unique genre in literature, detailing the history of Jesus as Messiah, Savior, and Lord. It is four accounts of one clarion gospel call. Paul describes the gospel in Corinthians.

> I passed on to you what was most important and what had also been passed on to me. Christ died for our sins, just as the Scriptures said. He was buried, and he was raised from the dead on the third day, just as the Scriptures said. (1 Corinthians 15.3-4, NLT)

The message of the cross is offensive to our pride, traditions, and philosophy. Paul recognized that the message of the cross was a "stumbling block" for the Jews and foolishness to Gentiles. Yet, Paul preached that Christ was crucified and that He saved those who believed. (cf. 1 Corinthians. 1.18,23)

The gospel is offensive to our modern sensibilities, just as people were offended by the message in ancient culture. The gospel offends the inadequacy of any self-justification before God. Until we recognize the depth of the offense of our sin before God, does the cross have real meaning? Yet, when we do, we can readily embrace that it is the power of God unto salvation to those who believe.

The Apostles were "thoroughly convinced" eyewitnesses of Christ. They followed him, heard his teaching, and watched his betrayal and death. Then the unthinkable happened. Jesus arose from the grave and appeared to them over 40 days with what Luke describes as "convincing truths." His appearances were their illumination that He came in fulfillment of both the law and the prophets. The disciples boldly proclaimed the good news of Jesus Christ as Messiah, Savior, and Lord.

The Gospel Fellowship

The revelation is that God makes believers to be gloriously one. Paul reminds believers of their togetherness in Christ. Jew and Gentile are gathered together 1.10, made alive 2.1, raised-up 2.6, fitly framed, and seated in heavenly places. Paul expands this theme as the epistle unfolds as the church is a new citizenship, household, and temple, as seen in the last chapter. The body of Christ consists of spiritual brothers and sisters in Christ. Paul brings a rich imagery of this unity of the grace gathering.

> Which in other ages was not made known unto the sons of men, as it is now revealed unto his holy apostles and prophets by the Spirit; That the Gentiles should be fellow heirs, and of the same body, and partakers of his promise in Christ by the gospel:
> (Ephesians 3. 5-7, KJBT)

Fellow – Heirs

Paul stresses the depth of this revelation that the believing Gentiles are fellow heirs, members, and partakers of God's promises. They had not become proselytes into a new religious system or converted from a different belief system. Rather. Paul uses the terms of the relationship and kinship. The new birth brings God's family together.

The grace gathering is heirs of the promise of the kingdom of God. Legally, heirs share the rights of the terms of the inheritance. His letter to Romans gives even more insight into the believer's heirship with Christ in God. (cf. Romans 8.16-17) Whatever is given by God the Father to His Son Christ also belongs to all who are in Christ. What a marvelous inheritance and glorious truth!

Fellow-Members

As fellow members rightly related to God and one another, believers share together in their Heavenly Father's impartial grace. Class distinctions or social division do not characterize Christ's community or the church's theology. The church is a beautiful gathering where everyone matters, including you!

Protecting the family name and personal honor was highly esteemed in the ancient Mediterranean culture. People married within the social class structure. Roman citizenship was coveted and enjoyed only by a few people. Divisions between the free class and the slave class were remarkable. The senatorial upper ruling class or the equestrian or decurion order had little interaction with the lower classes.[1]

The church had little social appeal. But the gospel broke through class barriers. There are no racial or ethnic divisions in the body of Christ. The power of the gospel brings believers together and transforms them into a new body. Therefore, Paul describes the grace gathered people as a body in Ephesians 4, with a unique oneness that transcends class, ethnicity, or being male or female. There is true equality of essence and being in the body of Christ. The superficial divisions in the world dissolve as the Spirit of God empowers His children to live as one. The grace-gathered children will love one another, just like their Heavenly Father loves them.

Fellow-Partakers

This new community of believers were indeed heirs of the promises of God. God's gracious gospel extends to everyone. The Holy Spirit indwells anyone who receives God's gift of salvation. Using the language of Paul in Romans, the Gentiles are "grafted into" God's family and equal participants in the grace-gathering. The church *ethos* is humility, and kingdom greatness is service. In the Roman Empire, the impoverished, slaves, and the upper ruling class were together as a new community.

Such a community was "radically" different in a world where conflict and division were the norm. The church loved one another. Just as there is equal footing at the cross, there is equal standing in the church. The grace gathering is grace-filled and exhibits the kingdom of light that brings people together. Paul had oversight of the gospel and the new community. It was the fullness of time in God's economy Paul recognized that he was created and called for such a time.

---

[1] Jeffers, James S. The Greco-Roman World of the New Testament Era, Exploring the Background of Early Christianity, IVP Academic, Downers Grove.

Paul the Minister

Paul did not pull his apostolic rank but referred to himself as a minister or *diakonos*–a servant. Jesus said that the greatest among you will be your minister or servant, Mark 10.45. The kingdom of heaven and light runs just the opposite of the kingdoms of this world that elevate prestige, power, and prominence. Paul was a simple servant, the least among them, the "chief of sinners" in his epistle to Romans. The servant of Jesus is a servant to the people he was equipping in the Faith.

> Of which I was made a minister, according to the gift of the grace of God given unto me by the effective working of his power. Unto me, who is less than the least of all saints, is this grace given, that I should preach among the Gentiles the unsearchable riches of Christ; And to make all men see what the fellowship of the mystery is, which from the beginning of the world has been hidden in God, who created all things by Jesus Christ: To the intent that now unto the principalities and powers in heavenly places might be known by the church the manifold wisdom of God. (Ephesians 3.7-10, KJBT)

The Face of the Gospel

Humility and service characterize the church. The gospel does not advance through arrogance, a sense of being an elitist club, or with people emulating the world in attitudes, desires, and methods. The gospel expands through humility and obedience to the king we serve. Humility makes the gospel attractive, and the world notices those who have been with Christ.

Humbly Serves

Paul's service was that he came bearing a gift from God to the Gentiles. It was the effective working of the power of Christ within him. Paul was honored to be the gift bearer in heralding the message in this grace gift. Paul was there to help unwrap the gift of grace that all men could see. These deep riches cannot be traced or ever fully comprehended. The gift of salvation by grace through faith is the gift that keeps giving.

Unsearchable Riches in Christ

Like the children's song, *Deep and Wide*, the fountain of salvation is incomprehensibly deep and expansively wide. His ministry was practically one of preaching and teaching, revealing the glorious mystery once hidden. God's glorious wisdom is on display among all of His creation, whether in heaven or earth.

Salvation is rich and vast and completed in Christ. Paul describes it as the eternal purpose carried out in Christ's life and work in verse 11, according to the eternal purpose of the Father.

Exalts the Name of Christ

Christ is a reference to the messianic role of Jesus. He is the "anointed one" described in the Old Testament, the fulfillment of the long-awaited promised Messiah. *Jesus* means the Lord is salvation. The Old Testament Hebrew equivalent is Joshua.

The angel told Mary that Jesus would save people from their sins-pointing to his humanity in the work of salvation. He is also Lord or (Kyrios). The title expresses honor and points to His divine role as Master of the universe. As Lord, He is the Creator of all things. The Lord denotes His sovereign and ultimate rule and reign as deity.

Conclusion

The truth of the gospel is freeing. Martin Luther discovered the gospel truth–the believer is "justified by faith." He was anxious over his sin, and his soul found freedom in the gospel. Rooted deeply in a new identity in Christ, his life changed and became a catalyst of change for many. These great truths were the essentials for the gospel of Christ and a defining moment in church history.

These five summary statements of theological conviction from the Reformation remain a concise tool for understanding salvation is by grace alone, through faith alone, in Christ alone, based upon Scripture alone, for the glory of God alone. The clear message of the gospel cuts through the fog of spiritual confusion. People often struggle with feelings they might not be "doing enough" for God's approval or acceptance. We subtly slide back into thinking that our salvation depends upon our performance. Our works are never sufficient and will never be for our salvation. Grace is about Christ's all-sufficient work done on our behalf. While suspended between heaven and earth, Jesus' final words before He died were "It is Finished". He meant it, so receive it!

*In this was manifested
the love of God toward us,
because God sent his only
begotten Son into the world,
that we might live through him.
In this is love,
not that we loved God,
but that he loved us,
and sent his Son to be
the atoning sacrifice
for our sins.*
(I John 4.9-10, KJBT)

A Prayer for God's Love

Heavenly Father,

I pray that your glorious and unlimited resources will invade my space and empower me with inner strength through your Holy Spirit. Every room in my heart is open to you today. You are my Lord!

I pray that spiritual roots will grow deeply in Christ until you are the total satisfaction of my heart. I desire to be strengthened and nourished in your deep reservoir of love.

I pray with all God's people that we will be enveloped completely, thoroughly saturated, and firmly established in Christ's surpassing love.

I turn from my sin and what has kept me indifferent to you. Rekindle my cold heart with Christ's love. Strengthen my heart in trust. I want to live most pleasing to you. I ask for the fullness of your life, and power will fill me, till all that I see is Jesus, until I see you face to face.

In Jesus' Loving Name. Amen

Praying for an Invasion of Love

Chapter Seven

Ephesians 3.13-20

It is refreshing to hear of spiritual awakenings happening all around and especially through the universities across America. Young college students are broken and hungry for meaning and purpose in life. Many are turning to God! Worship, singing, prayers, intercession, confession, repentance of sin, and turning once again to Christ and His love as the source of satisfaction. My prayer is that this sweeps across our nation.

There has never been a more desperate time spiritually in the American church. We needed a return to Christ. A loss of our upward gaze upon the glory of Christ has bred spiritual apathy and heartless worship. Oh, how we have been drifting away from our love and passion for Christ. I pray for a remnant of people with a spiritual hunger who seek Christ and long for fellowship. Adrift on the tumultuous seas of this world, they desire to swim in the depths of God's love.

Why do nations drift for moral foundations? Why do churches drift from their once passion for Christ? The songwriter caught the sentiment when he penned, Prone to wander Lord, I feel it, prone to leave the God I love. Why do believers find themselves adrift at times? When there is a drifting from God, it stands to reason there is a drifting from love. The internal coldness of the heart is devastating to the message of Christ and the body life of the church.

Without love, misunderstandings broaden, division deepens, chasms widen, and offense abounds. Loneliness is beside you; anxiety accompanies you, dreadful uncertainty before you, and fears settle deep within. Rejection of self and others becomes a miserable friend. The shores of love seem so distant for those adrift.

Love is the longing of every heart. That's why fractured relationships hurt us deeply. So, we build walls to protect us from more hurt. In isolation and alienation, torments of guilt, shame, unforgiveness, and resentment thrive. We create our form of internal hell.

In the depths of despair, you cry out, Why God? God seems silent. It seems that God does not care. Emotional hurts can run very deep. So deep that words are unhelpful. God sits with us in silence and reaches us with a nail-pierced hand. His scars speak loudly of His love.

If you peel back the layers of why we drift, love for God is the core issue. The heart of Paul's prayer is the depth of the need. Love brings understanding, love brings together, and love is an unbreakable tie that binds. What if we began praying for an invasion of love in ourselves and others? We might find our brokenness healed by His love and our lives revived by a passion for Christ.

Revival is a hunger in which Christ meets our innermost needs, His presence becomes the ultimate satisfaction, and His love for others motivates our highest aspirations.

Our Great Access

Christ offers access to the Father, even in our deepest hunger. His throne room is a rich treasure of love and provision. Paul's beautiful spirit-directed prayer is insightful in understanding what a life filled with passion for Christ looks like. He prays for the empowering presence of Christ that deepens and strengthens believers, with His indwelling that secures us in love and operates in our lives.

> In whom we have boldness and access with confidence by the faith in him. Therefore, I ask you not to be discouraged by my tribulations for you, which is your glory. For this cause I bow my knees unto the Father of our Lord Jesus Christ, From whom the whole family in heaven and earth is named, (Ephesians 3.12-14, KJBT)

Notice what the believer possesses. We have bold access to the Father in prayer with assurance that we are received. The imputed righteousness of Christ is our ticket. Once an enemy of God is now a friend of God. God is approachable through receiving His undeserved gracious favor. Our access brings us confidence. Humility and cheerful courage accompany the heart that can bring requests before God with boldness.

Hebrews describes the superiority of Christ as our Great High Priest, "Let us therefore come boldly to the throne of grace, that we may obtain mercy and find grace to help in time of need." (Hebrews 4.16, NKJV)

Let's look a little deeper into Paul's prayer.

A Strengthen Inner Man

How often do you feel weak or unsure because of life's circumstances? Pray the Holy Spirit invades the inner man with strength (vss. 14-16). Jesus is neither perplexed by our weakness nor our struggles.

Paul bowed his knees in intercessory prayer for believers. The believer has the empowering presence of Christ working in his behalf. Herein is personal godliness and love through God's empowering Spirit.

> For this cause I bow my knees unto the Father of our Lord Jesus Christ, From whom the whole family in heaven and earth is named, That he would grant you, according to the riches of his glory, to be strengthened with might by his Spirit in the inner man;
> (Ephesians 3. 14-16, KJBT)

From the Richness of His Glory

God's throne is glorious! His riches are vast and massive. His storehouse is full. His perfect gifts flow from His good. Spiritual blessings await those who ask, seek, and knock. He desires to bless his children out of His great love.

We often pray for surface-level things only. We pray for physical healing, financial situations, a better job, or the need of someone we love. Our prayers sometimes only scratch the surface of circumstances. Notice that Paul asked that there would be empowerment in the inner man. What does He mean?

The Inside-Out Life

The Christian life operates from the inside out. It is easy to go through the motions of religion without heartfelt devotion. Such can also happen collectively in the gathering and the larger culture. Historians write about spiritual awakenings that have revived passionless believers in the past. One such revival occurred in the 1700's.

Our pilgrim forefathers had sailed to America. They were fleeing persecution and pursuing liberty of worship. As the generation of the original settlers passed the scene, their children and grandchildren became focused on nation-building, wealth, and material things. The once strong witness of their fathers had drifted into a spiritual malaise that paralyzed their Christian witness. They were spiritually asleep. They had forgotten why their forefathers traversed these shores and wrote the Mayflower Compact in 1620. Their love for Christ was cold.

Some thirty years after penning Ephesians, John records Jesus' calling to the Seven Churches in Revelation 2 & 3. Jesus addresses deeper spiritual issues of the inner man. Jesus commended them for their orthodoxy, but their hearts were dry and passionless. They left their first love. Repentance and returning to their first love was the remedy.

Aligning your heart with the heart of the Father is critical for loving God with all your heart, soul, mind, and strength. The inner man is important in Paul's teaching.[1] Both the Jewish and Gentile believers would have generally understood the concepts. Christians should align the mind (being shaped by the world and prompted by the sinful nature) with the truth of Scripture. Paul called for a renewal of the mind, being transformed and not conforming to the patterns of the world. (cf. Romans 12.1-2) Paul rightly places much emphasis on thinking God's thoughts.

> Finally, brethren, whatever things are true, whatever things *are* noble, whatever things *are* just, whatever things *are* pure, whatever things *are* lovely, whatever things *are* of good report, if *there is* any virtue and if *there is* anything praiseworthy—meditate on these things.   (Philippians 4.8, NKJV)

---

[1] See Thayers, "The internal, inner man, i. e. the soul, conscience."

The inside-out life of the believer means that truth shapes the mind, and obedience is the mark of the Christian walk. The Christian then conforms his walk and habits through the virtuous disciplines of private devotion, public worship, communion, and serving opportunities. All are motivated by a heart devoted to Christ. Such a life informs the conscience, shapes our character, and brings positive emotional change. If you are looking to change how you feel, this is how it happens in the Christian life.

No wonder Paul made this his prayer. We need strength in the inner man because most of our problems have deeper spiritual roots. It can be our prayer for glorious, unlimited resources from the storehouse of the Father. It is not only an inheritance belonging to us for the future but a reservoir of strength from the Father of love now. Paul's prayer is a template for praying for one another, your children, a loved one, and yourself.

Rooted & Grounded in Love

The Holy Spirit empowers believers and takes up residence with the believer. The indwelling presence of Christ gives us a wonderful communion of abiding in the Father's. "That Christ may dwell in your hearts by faith, that you, being rooted and grounded in love" vs. 3.17.

Paul wants the church to understand this indwelling love. They become rooted and grounded in the truth of God's love for them in Christ. God makes His home in our hearts. He explained to the Corinthians that we are the temple that God indwells. Circumstances can leave you feeling unsettled. God does not "vacate the premises" with our trying circumstances. No, God is present.

We have already explored the mind, emotions, and will as an aspect of the inner man. For our purposes here, I want us to explore the heart as the seat of our passion, desires, affections, purpose, and endeavors. The word heart *kardia* is very much like the concept of inner man we looked at previously.[2]

These aspects of the inner man are often the motivation and drive within us. Paul asks that our hearts become thoroughly grounded with

---

[2] See Thayers Heart – kardia -" the fountain and seat of the thoughts, passions, desires, appetites, affections, purposes, endeavors"

roots, founded, established, and firm. So, Paul is praying that your *soul* draws deeply from God's reservoir of love. Spiritual nourishment is in Christ. As your spiritual roots grow deeper in His love, you become established in a satisfying and sustaining strength. The Apostle John said it well through such an initiating love. It is not that we first loved Him, but that He first loved us and gave His life.

> In this is love, not that we loved God, but that he loved us, and sent his Son to be the atoning sacrifice for our sins. Beloved, if God so loved us, we also ought to love one another. (1 John 4.10-11, KJBT)

God's *agape* love is sacrificial and self-giving. It is the ultimate and purest love. It meets the deepest longing of the heart, and it is the highest ethic of living. The world drinks from broken cisterns that never satisfy. They pursue *eros* and center their passions around this, and their desires are motivated by the sinful nature led by inordinate affections.

Others seek to center their lives in family-love *storego* or friends *phileo*, without agape. They sabotage relationships by placing unrealistic expectations upon others to fulfill emotional needs. When God's love forms our passions and endeavors, we love others as Jesus loves. As such, we become rooted down to face troubles and become a marvelous display of his love.

The Fullness of God

Paul wanted the Ephesian believers to know the incomprehensible display of love as a breadth, length, depth, and height. His love passes knowledge is far greater than we can imagine, and yet it is there for the believer to lay hold of. The fullness of God is available and operative in Christ. He is the fullness of God.

> May be able to comprehend with all saints what is the breadth, and length, and depth, and height; And to know the love of Christ, which passes knowledge, that you might be filled with all the fullness of God.
> (Ephesians 3. 18-19, KJBT)

Paul prays that they would understand and experience the limitless dimension of love. Look down, stand firm on love's firm foundation. Look up to the sky, and there is a boundless love for the grasping. Turn to your right and left, and see God's love, being surrounded by it. God's love surpasses what your mind can comprehend, but it is a love meant to be known by experience. God's love meets the depth of the soul's need in the most satisfying way.

What if you opened your heart to let Jesus love you in the bitterness of betrayal? What if there was an invasion of love that so fills you that misunderstandings cease, broken relationships mended, and unforgiveness released? The depth of God's riches in love always surpasses the depth of any personal need, whatever that need may be.

Jesus stands in the midst of His church. He strengthens and satisfies with nothing less than His presence. The believer has everything he needs in Christ. From this prayer, we gain guidance on how to pray for spiritual growth. It also shapes believers as the kingdom of light that penetrates spiritual darkness. Pray for yourself, your children, the church, and all others. God might just move with a massive outpouring of His love!

Conclusion

When God invades our space, then love moves in. Jonathan Edwards described the awakening experience as involving a deep love for Christ and joy in Northampton and the colonies. From spiritual apathy and indifference arose a new spiritual vitality. His *Treatise Concerning Religious Affections* described a renewed interest in personal purity, Scripture reading, and Christ's love within people. An awakened heart awakens to love.

Marvel in the magnificent Christ our Savior. He is glorious in the richness of the mystery of salvation.

Pray for an invasion of love! May His Holy love invade hearts, families, homes, churches, communities, schools, leaders, and nations. May our friends, neighbors, and even our enemies be swept up in the power of God's invading love!

Declare God's loving benedictions along with the Apostle Paul.

Now unto him who is able to do exceedingly abundantly above all that we ask or think, according to the power that works in us, Unto him be glory in the church by Christ Jesus throughout all ages, world without end. Amen.
(Ephesians 3.20-21, KJBT)

Look how these Christians love one another.
~ Tertullian

Radical Love Lived Out

Chapter Eight

Ephesians 4.1-10

What the world needs today is the love of Jesus! Most are unaware of either the depth of their brokenness or the desperation of their spiritual condition. In Jesus' time, the self-righteous could not see the depth of their sin. They assumed that their morality and religious activity would merit God's approval. These works-oriented people were offended by Jesus. But those who recognized their spiritual destitution powerfully encountered God's love.

The love of Jesus rocked the first-century world because broken people saw the love of the Heavenly Father like they had never seen before, and demons trembled in the spiritual realm. Such love was so compelling people flocked to him, turning from their sin and rebellion by receiving such love. They encountered a gracious love both uncommon and rare.

People are attracted to a church filled with the love of Jesus. The world takes note of people who have been with Jesus. Such a congregation is characterized by *grace and truth*, just like Jesus. It is a delicate balance for us, but Jesus lived it perfectly. Such a radical love deliberately lived out is life changing.

Traveling through the villages, Jesus' disciples laid aside their occupations to follow this peripatetic Rabbi. It was a unique opportunity to observe the gracious operation of the Kingdom of Heaven in temples, homes, countryside, and streets. It was the ultimate experience in hands-on learning. Walking in His steps, the disciples learned the core values, mission, message, and methods of Jesus and His kingdom.

They discovered that at the heart of Jesus was His passion for the Father's will and glory expressed sacrificially for people. So, Jesus often risked His reputation by eating with sinners, touching the unclean, and healing lepers. Jesus did not become like the world to win the world, but He did not shun sinners either. Neither did He "soft pedal" warning people of their sinful nature that is destructive. He always went straight for the heart with the good news

He showed the world desperate for real love what such a love looked like. He was God's love embodied in the flesh. His incarnation was God's grace on full display–an invasion of love. Many rejected and looked suspiciously upon such a love, but as many as received Him became the children of God. The early church understood they were called to imitate their Father's love, just like Jesus.

A Worthy Walk

Paul was writing to such a diverse group of believers in Ephesus. Many from the Jewish mono-theistic and legalistic backgrounds to the pleasure-seeking Greeks and those who had once been devoted worshipers at pagan temples. Many may have found themselves excluded from the marketplace because they would not pay homage to the emperor by burning incense at the marketplace entrance.[1]

The challenge before the church is "being in the world, but not of the world." The first century was no different. Christians would have experienced suffering for confessing Jesus as their Lord. Ephesus was not a supportive environment for godly living or walking as Jesus walked. Wickedness was pervasive, but there they were to live out what Paul describes as a "worthy walk."

> I, therefore, the prisoner of the Lord, beseech you that you walk worthy of the calling to which you are called, With all lowliness and meekness, with longsuffering, forbearing one another in love; Endeavoring to keep the unity of the Spirit in the bond of peace. There is one body, and one Spirit, even as you are called in one hope of your calling; One Lord, one faith, one baptism, One God, and Father of all, who is above all, and through all, and in you all. (Ephesians 4.1-6 KJBT)

---

[1] See Endnotes link, Joseph Stowell, Ephesus: The Seven Churches of Revelation, Our DailyBread- The Days of Discovery, Video Documentary.

This section of Paul's ethical teaching aligns very well with Jesus' words on the Sermon on the Mount and His words: *"Blessed are the peacemakers."* The children of God live out this radical love as peacemakers. Humility is a Christian virtue.

Humility

They should walk in "lowliness of mind" rather than self-centered living. Relationships require humility. Being in harmony with the Maker is the ground for harmonious relationships. Unity is the earmark of the worthy walk. The disciples struggled with both humility and unity. They fell into the subtle trap of selfish ambition. They sought prominence in Jesus' kingdom work.

Human pride is the unfortunate motivation for disputes, disunity, and relational heartache. As the disciples argued, Jesus humbly exampled service as the virtue of Kingdom greatness. The right attitude is essential for anyone to live in harmony with others.

Lowliness of mind or humility derives from rightly seeing yourself in light of how God sees you. It is having a humble opinion of self in relationship to God and others. Egoism, pride, and boastful arrogance are not kingdom virtues. Our era nurtures selfish individualism and even promotes it. The Spirit of the age is narcissistic. The cult of self has captured the day, and the "selfie" proves it! It's our life and our happiness at stake, we think.

False humility is often self-debasing and masks pride. True humility embraces one's new position in Christ with gratitude and aligns the mind with the truth. It enables confident living. When the believer conforms his thinking and self-worth to Christ, the Christian life becomes a joy-filled relationship.

Living for the pleasure and will of His Father was forefront in Christ's thinking. *Do nothing from selfishness or empty conceit, but with humility of mind let each regard one another as more important than himself.* (Philippians 2.31 NKJV). Make the shape of your words grace-filled and humble. Humility leads to gratitude, thankfulness, and authentic worship before God.

Walk of Meekness

Meekness is an honorable spiritual virtue. It is bringing the power of self under the control of the Holy Spirit, given over to Christ for His glory. It is facing life circumstances as Jesus faced them in the Garden of Gethsemane. He yielded his will to the will of the Heavenly Father. Such a yieldedness unfolds as the struggle of agonizing prayer.

The meek soul is occupied more with God and less with self. The meek embrace the inward work of grace that is sustaining in the face of life's difficulties.[2] Accepting what God permits in our lives is sometimes difficult. His vast and endless grace sustains believers through hardship and difficulties. Jesus said the meek shall inherit the earth. Meekness is not being weak. It is the yielding of oneself to the Holy Spirit's empowering presence and exchanging weakness for the strength of Christ.

Walk of Patience

The walk worthy of the Lord is a patient attitude in dealing with people. Patience does not mean we subject ourselves to abusive, unhealthy situations or dangerous environments. But it does mean we choose not to retaliate when wronged in relationships. We offer forgiveness. In doing so, we release ourselves from the bitterness of the offense and release the offender to God.

Jesus even extended forgiveness for those crucifying him. He was longsuffering. Jesus' response was temperate and self-restrained. Longsuffering means possessing an inward governance by the Holy Spirit, while impatience and domination are fleshly motivated responses to life situations. One submitted to Christ is self-controlled through difficult circumstances. It is the fruit of the Holy Spirit operative available to believers daily. (cf. Galatians 6.22)

Misunderstandings, conflict, and differences describe the best of friendships at times. Growing in Christ is growing in grace. The grace where we find ourselves accepted before God is the grace that we extend in relationships. So, believers in Christ bear under one another

---

[2] See. W. E. Vine, Vine's *Expository Dictionary of New Testament Words*, "Meekness", 727- 728.

in love and acceptance because of the bond of Christ. So, living in harmony chooses restraint over "short-fused" responses.

A Unified Walk

Harmonious relationships mean walking in peace. Believers should keep unity and guard peace–quickly and with zeal. "Endeavor" means to "make haste with zeal." Urgent in Paul's thinking was the unity of the church. It needs attention immediately. This relational tidying up is necessary for unity. We would use hyperbole and say, "Bust a gut" or "Break a leg" to keep the unity of the Spirit.

Peace is the believer's bond living in a unified love. Believers cannot create peace, but it is the fruit of the Spirit flowing from love. It is this radical love that the body of Christ lives out.

Walking as One

In the previous verses, Paul has described the characteristics of living in harmony with one another. He points to the theological foundation that characterizes a new way of living. The new community of the grace gathering includes the multi-ethnic, multicultural people brought together in the person of Christ. They are one. A unified church is the answer to Jesus' prayer in John 17.

> There is one body, and one Spirit, even as you are called in one hope of your calling; One Lord, one faith, one baptism, One God, and Father of all, who is above all, and through all, and in you all. (Ephesians 4.1-6, KJBT)

One Body in One Spirit

There is One Body of Christ, called the church universal, and Christ is the head of this church. As a fully functional living body, Paul's analogy of the church is that of a body. The church is God's living organism operating in the world. The church's unity is a witness to the world that God is alive and at work through love. There are many parts to a physical body, but the body functions harmoniously for God's purposes on earth. Paul gives detailed teaching in 1 Corinthians 12 about the functioning of the spiritually gifted body for deeper study.

Like God breathing life into Adam in the Creation of Adam, the Holy Spirit breathes life into His new creation. There is a dynamic spiritual vibrancy in a healthy church. More than mere stirred-up emotions, it is consistent growth in Christ.

This supernatural work in God's people is the work of the Holy Spirit that empowers believers in Christlikeness and magnifies Christ. The body of Christ stands as His people (chosen, holy, special) who declare the praises of Christ as a royal priesthood in the world. (cf. 1 Peter 2.9)

The dynamic operation of God's empowering life within the church enables the spirit-filled walk. The body of Christ is built up by the spiritual gifts exercised in ministry and sharing the gospel. God's Spirit convicts the lost of their sin, brings the spiritually dead to life, and baptizes and indwells believers at salvation.

Our hearts gladly celebrate the great love of God in worship. The Spirit consecrates and empowers believers to walk in Christ and be the conduit of His ongoing work until He returns. Jesus declared that the gates of hell cannot prevail against the church. The life of God is flowing through her by the Holy Spirit.

One Hope

The grace-gathered new creation belongs to Jesus! Jesus builds His church. Our confident expectation in the gospel of Christ is our only real hope. A glorious preservation and fulfillment awaits the body held in the domain of a desperate world. But Jesus, who is our hope, is also our battle champion. He gives strength for the battle and the promise of victory. Jesus never fails, and He does not lose.

The church deals with detractors, decrying the hypocrisy (sometimes rightfully so), irrelevance, or absurdity of the church and its message. The gospel advances through its preaching. Even in the most oppressive regions around the globe, the gospel penetrates. The early church persevered through persecution and even withstood the infiltration of heresy and false teaching.

Jesus stands to strengthen those experiencing persecution across the world today. Jesus conquered death, hell, and the grave. Christ's death, burial, and resurrection are the very foundation of our one faith. He strengthens his people in the greatest hope!

One Lord, Faith & Baptism

The Ancient Eastern culture centered around family honor. One's identity was in the family name, and bringing shame to the family name was avoided at all costs. Modern Western culture centers around the individual. Personal happiness, success, and fulfillment are self-derived, leading to an endless pursuit of empty things, just like the writer of Ecclesiastes elucidates.

Moral bankruptcy, the marginalization of God, and a massive spiritual vacuum characterize modern culture. The church possesses an abundance of spiritual wealth. Her mode of operation rests in the eternal, magnifying God and walking in the fullness of the Spirit. In other words, the grace gathering isn't man-centered, need-oriented in focus. The church is uniquely a Christ-centered and Christ-focused gathering.

Jesus is the Lord *Kyrios* of the Church. He is preeminent in the church's existence and operation. Jesus has first place in our lives and the church. He is Master and Lord! He is the proper object of the Faith. We often wrongly assume that the church centers around programs, preachers, worship styles, precepts, slick slogans, or what we are against or denominational affiliation or cultural identity.

The church of Jesus Christ belongs to Him. His kingdom supersedes what concerns this world. He is our unchanging identity in a world that seeks to mold us in their image or conform our message to the world's narratives. It is a constant danger that our faith becomes founded upon what we see, need, or external pressure rather than Christ and His Word.

The body of Christ has one Lord and one Faith. Faith here is a confession of certain beliefs concerning Christ and the gospel. The early church had a similar faith and practice concerning the person of Christ, salvation, and walking holy before the Lord. Christ is the only proper object of our faith. Faithfulness is the by-product of being saved by grace through faith in Christ.

Setting our lives apart unto Christ is also the sanctifying work of faith lives. It leads to a glorious unity of the faith (Ephesians 4.13). Faith is not an inwardly contrived inspirational feeling. Faith is the proper response to hearing the truth of Scripture through obedience.

Baptism is the initial act of consecration. It is an outward indication of God's grace and the response of faith. One Baptism was the covenant sign of being in Christ and a part of the covenant community through the Holy Spirit. Baptism is an outward testimony of the believer's co-identification with Christ and God's gracious work in the heart. The believer's baptism is in the unified name of the Triune God (Father, Son, Holy Spirit). (cf. Matthew 28.19)

Partakers of the new covenant are resting in Christ's assurance. The new community is known as being baptized into His death, burial, and resurrection. Arising from the watery grave, they set forward to walk in the newness of life. (1 Corinthians 12.13, Romans 6.3-4) Belonging to the Lord, we have our place in His body because He is the Lord of life. Paul beautifully sums up our life in Romans 14:8-9: *For whether we live, we live unto the Lord; and whether we die, we die unto the Lord: whether we live therefore, or die, we are the Lords.*

God's Oneness

Paul rounds out the foundation of this sevenfold oneness with God. God is the foundation, and Paul describes Him in the most tender relational terms. He is Father. In His omnipotence, He is working in every part of our lives. Just as there is unity in the Trinity, God works relationally through His body. The Father's work in the body is a unifying work of faith under the headship of Christ. Christ is over it all.

Christ is Over All

The relevance of the church is either downplayed or disparaged today because of its imperfections. The church is not perfect, and not every church is healthy. But remember, the church belongs to Christ alone, and in a healthy church, the gathering is growing in submission and conformity to Christ as the Head of the Church. The church's purpose is to conform us to the image of Christ. Our imperfections only reveal areas to consider for His renewing work.

> But unto every one of us is given grace according to the measure of the gift of Christ. Therefore, he said, When he ascended on high, he led captivity captive, and gave gifts unto men. (Now that he ascended, what is it but that he also descended first into the lower parts of the

earth? He who descended is also the same who ascended far above all heavens, that he might fill all things.)   (Ephesians 4. 7-10, KJBT)

Just how powerful is the head of the church? Jesus graces the church with Himself—His very presence. His presence is so pervasive. The cross was the triumph of Jesus because of the resurrection. Jesus was exalted and vindicated as righteous by being raised from the dead and His ascension on high. "He disarmed the spiritual rulers and authorities. He shamed them publicly by his victory over them on the cross". (cf. Colossians. 2.15) Christ's Lordship over all things, Jesus announces judgment over the kingdom of darkness, Satan, sin, and death.

Jesus ascended far above heaven! His presence fills all things! He fills the grace-gathered church with nothing less than Himself. His church is empowered not only with harmony but also glorious unity. Every knee shall bow in every realm, whether heaven or earth, confessing His Lordship.

Radical Love Lived-Out

Every domain is under His Lordship. The church has been given the "keys to the kingdom" and spiritual authority. Radical love lived out then is the recognition that God is at work in the world through His church. These virtues encourage healthy family and personal relationships and make good employer-employee relationships. Such love lives also sacrificially in ministry to others.

The early church lived this way in their world filled with broken relationships. Tertullian said, "Look how these Christians love one another." They made history by caring for widows and orphans. They especially cared for unwanted children abandoned in the marketplace, rescuing them from being sold into slavery.

They buried the poor who could not afford proper burial because they believed that human beings were in the image of God. God's love made a radical difference in their lives. They simply lived it out. In actuality, it is not that radical. It's normal Christianity. Our challenge is to live out this good news in the broken sectors of the world today. The world notices sacrificial love.

*I can't change the bad things I've done.
I can't relive the victories I've won.
But, I can be a vessel of grace!*

*I can't undo the wrong I've committed
I can't redo the good things omitted
But, I can be a vessel of grace!*

*I can't change those moments of sin.
I can't make things how I wish they had been.
But, I can be a vessel of grace!*

*I will choose to love without condition.
I will choose to trust without suspicion.
Because I am a vessel of grace!*

*No Matter what my lot in life,
From the depths of my pain and strife.
I will be a vessel of grace!*

~ Pastor Bud Beverly

The Anatomy of a Disciple

Chapter Nine

Ephesians 4.14-23

Hurrying to biology class one morning, a pre-med student and friend saw me passing by the human anatomy lab. He knew I was not particularly inclined to biology even though the discipline fascinated me. Crunching numbers was more my thing. I reluctantly entered the lab upon his insistence. He was teaching a lesson on the human heart he had been dissecting. I saw firsthand what I had only seen in pictures. I reluctantly thanked him and quickly escaped the lab.

Taking a minute to gain my composure, I hurried to biology class. As I sat in class, I reflected on the whole scenario and then about my own heart lying unseen and unnoticed in my chest. The human body's order, complexity, structure, and function remain fascinating. The vast functioning of the human body is unseen. That is why physicians probe, ask questions, draw blood, and take scans and images when you are ill.

Since my childhood, I have been a part of church life. Church has helped shape my life and has been a source of joy. There are hours of behind-the-scenes preparations underlying the observable. Spiritual gifts are the vital organs that function in a healthy church. Jesus ascended and descended, and he gave gifts to men.

The purpose of the church is the dynamic function of clearly presenting the gospel so that hearers may **ENTER** a life-changing relationship with Christ, EMBRACE their place in the body of Christ, build up one another, and become **EQUIPPED** through Bible-Based, Christ-centered teaching, training them to serve Christ in the world. We hope this process is ongoing in every person in our fellowship at Glamorgan Chapel. It's our mode of assimilation. The healthy church is a disciple-making community.

A Disciple-Making Community

Jesus's followers were called disciples. A disciple is a student and learner who follows the teachings of his rabbi. Paul identifies four essential parts of a functioning and healthy disciple and the environment of such a disciple-making congregation. The church's temperament and emphasis shape the disciples' character. Paul says as much, in verses 7-11:

> And he gave some, apostles; and some, prophets; and some, evangelists; and some, pastors and teachers; For the perfecting of the saints, for the work of the ministry, for the edifying of the body of Christ: Until we all come in the unity of the faith, and of the knowledge of the Son of God, unto a spiritually mature man, unto the measure of the stature of the fullness of Christ:
> (Ephesians 4.11-13, KJBT)

A healthy disciple-making community prioritizes Scripture as truth, and the congregation is healthy in love for God and one another. Sound and clear biblical teaching and life application preaching remain a critical function of the church. Engaging in Christ-centered worship, praying together, and a fellowship that ministers to the care of one another through prayer. The church reaches outside her walls to share the good news so others may join the disciple-making process.

In essence, the gathering builds up one another and encourages maturity in Christlikeness. The church follows hard after Christ. It is a community committed to building itself in love.

A Bible Teaching Community

Notice the foundational gifts are the apostles of Christ. An apostle was not self-appointed but was one of the twelve eyewitnesses to the resurrected Christ. The body grew in fellowship around the preaching of the gospel and the apostle's doctrine. (cf. Acts 2.42) Prophets were the bold proclaimers of the truth. They also gave spirit-directed instruction. Evangelists are easy to spot because they seek opportunities to share the gospel. Then there is the role of pastor-teachers. They care for the body of Christ like a shepherd care for sheep. They help the gathering by teaching the Scripture and shepherding the flock in the truth.

The pastor-teacher, along with the other gifts, is given for the maturing believers into Christlikeness, equipping them to do the work of the ministry. A healthy, maturing body does not depend upon the pastor to solely minister to the enormity of the concerns within the church body. That is unbiblical and the cause of a great deal of ministry burnout. The pastor equips the gathering to minister as Christ unto one another.

With the involvement and the diverse use of spiritual gifts, the soil for growth cultivates maturity. The early church gives us the model. The deacon serves the practical needs of the congregation while the apostles and pastors labored in the Word of God and prayer. (Acts 6.1) The result was fantastic. God added to the body of Christ.

A Disciple is Becoming Equipped

A Bible-teaching environment then focuses on teaching sound doctrine. Like the Berean Christians, the New Testament disciple is learning the essential Bible doctrines of the church such as theology proper, Christ, Holy Spirit, Bible, man, salvation, church, and end times. Paul taught the Ephesian believers both publicly and privately. He taught them from house to house and often in tears.

Paul would not only have taught the doctrines but would teach them how to see Christ through the lens of the Old Testament and apply their heart in obedience to the truth. Believing that the Bible is the Word of God without error or falsehood, our faith's foundation rests on the coherent and consistent trues of Scripture. The Christian life is believable as it is lived consistently in the Christ-centered life.

Serving Hands

God gives gifts for serving the Body of Christ. It is the work of *deacons* serving. Being a member is not spectatorial but as one actively involved and engaged in the body of Christ. Christian worship, life, and ministry are always participatory. Like Jesus' early followers, the modern-day disciple is an intense, hands-on learning experience.

Being sent out in ministry, we are called servants of the Most High God in the world. We are servant leaders in a world that views leadership as authority, power, and control. The works of church ministry happen both inside and outside the walls.

A Disciple Builds Up the Body

Discipleship is not a Christianized self-help program of self-actualization. Christian discipleship is Christ-formation. It is being human the way God intended it. It is a direct focus on building up God's kingdom through the work of a local church.

Your salvation involves a personal relationship with Christ because this is only the beginning. It involves meaningful connections and active involvement that build up one another. It is impossible to build up one another without a deliberate attempt to be involved in the body-life of the church. Those providentially hindered in attending should stay connected through relational contacts or following online services. Building up the body means utilizing our gifts as worship unto Christ.

Christ-Centered Fullness

So, a Bible teaching environment leads to unity within the graced gathering of people and growing in the experiential knowledge of the Lord. These early disciples were growing personally and corporately together. They were growing in their mind and spirit in the fullness of Christ and Christ's service. For a vibrant Christian life find a place to serve in ministry.

The body life of the church is multi-layered opportunities of service. From facility care and maintenance to teaching a class or participating on a worship team, ministry to the lonely, sick, or bereaved are active church ministries. Wherever there is brokenness, heartaches, suffering, or joy and happiness, the body of Christ is present.

Young married couples and those in struggling marriages all need the Christ-centered fullness of His work through the body of Christ. No matter one's age or situation in life, the church expresses Christ's presence among them. Christ's fullness may encourage and strengthen, direct and guide. The church is a dynamic ministry to people's ongoing needs in some capacity.

The fullness of Christ in worship is a great joy. Fellowship events that connect you relationally and grow in family life. The church is an ongoing advocate and support in prayer and practical ways. Some folks wait for a "sign in life" for purpose, direction, and guidance. You might be surprised that it's the church sign outside the building.

A Fellowship Growing in Christlikeness

The grace-gathering grows in fellowship that focuses on becoming like Christ. Believers encourage and stir each other to be like Jesus. People on the periphery or outside the church take note of a church filled with love and truth.

The healthy church does not center on celebrities, personalities, programs, or shows. The church is not an event. It is Christ's body demonstrating Christ's life in the world. That is attractive and healthy. A broken world needs to see a strong church growing up in love. It makes the gospel believable!

> We should no longer be children, tossed to and fro and carried about with every wind of doctrine, by the trickery of men, in the cunning craftiness of deceitful plotting, but, speaking the truth in love, may grow up in all things into Him who is the head—Christ— from whom the whole body, joined and knit together by what every joint supplies, according to the effective working by which every part does its share, causes growth of the body for the edifying of itself in love.
> (Ephesians 5.14-16, KJBT)

The church is a fellowship. Notice the terms Paul uses in verse 16 as a "whole body, joined and knit together. "Another New Testament word to describe this dynamic is *koinonia* or fellowship. The idea is a communion that comes together and works together in life experiences. It is a communion where Christ is the head, and the Holy Spirit operates.

Western culture has drifted far away from any sacred, transcending moral authority. Moral confusion and chaos result. With such pervasive disintegration, a biblical view of life, gender, sexuality, marriage, and family is not only questioned but readily rejected. It is the loss of the sacred. Human suffering deepens. Unhappiness, dissatisfaction, and growing mental and emotional health concerns loom large. The church has a crucial role in ministry to the brokenness in this suffering world, but in preserving the sacred in a secular world. Human suffering deepens as a result.

A Disciple is Growing in Truth and Love

A pervasive skepticism prevails. In secular culture, truth is determined either socially or subjectively and self-derived. Christ's church stands alone as the only community that upholds objective truth. The Bible is sacred, and its message is philosophically and logically consistent and corresponds to life.

A Love for Truth

A healthy disciple has a growing hunger for God's Word. Christ's disciples anchor in the truth of Scripture. Being anchored in the doctrines of Christ creates spiritual stability. Any "new revelation" or religious fad does not unsettle those settled in Scripture. The grace-gathered people anchor down in its love for truth.

Growing in the truth also enables discernment of those who desire scathing-off disciples to themselves rather than Christ. Unbiblical concepts are often shrouded in biblical language and redefined to suit false doctrines they wish to promote. A disciple's love for Christ brings self-centered ambitions in check and Christ as the preeminent one.

A disciple in the making is growing in the Lord through the body of Christ. The Apostle Peter gives both a warning and an admonition to grow spiritually.

> Therefore, [let me warn you] beloved, knowing these things beforehand, be on your guard so that you are not carried away by the error of unprincipled men [who distort doctrine] and fall from your own steadfastness [of mind, knowledge, truth, and faith], but grow [spiritually mature] in the grace and knowledge of our Lord and Savior Jesus Christ. To Him be glory (honor, majesty, splendor), both now and to the day of eternity. Amen.   (2 Peter 3.17-18, AMP)

Christ lived in the perfect balance of grace and truth (cf. John 1.7). Growing spiritually balanced is so important. Truth without grace leads to spiritual harshness. The Ephesian church was orthodox in doctrine but cold and heartless in practice. (cf. Revelation 3) They were to repent and return to their first love. Grace without truth leads to a church that surrenders her prophetic voice to the whims of culture. The compromising church must repent to retain its voice in culture.

Love Lived-Out in Relationships

Love is the relational aspect of the grace-gathered community. It is a cohesion that brings the disciple to live out love. It is grace lived out. We forgive others to the same extent as we receive and understand the depth of God's forgiveness in our lives. We extend grace in proportion to the grace received in our lives. A growing disciple yields daily to Christ the fullness of His life. The walk empowered by the Holy Spirit is one where the fruit of the Spirit (love, joy, peace, longsuffering, patience, self-control, patience, and goodness) nourishes the body.

A Disciple Follows the Steps of Christ in Obedience

Finally, the believer's walk is worthy of Christ, together in love, but it is a renewed walk in the Lord. We walk out our righteous position in Christ by being set apart to live unto Christ in a wicked and dark world. That is the light that shines in the darkness. Paul expresses it as a command to not walk like the Gentiles.

The church loses its testimony and relevance when it attempts to be like the world. The church lives out the kingdom of God among the kingdoms of men. It is light, love, and truth that penetrates the spiritual darkness. The world may or may not embrace or even like the church, but the world needs the church. The church supports a moral standard that strengthens the personal conscience, strengthens families, and supports a stable functioning culture.

> This I say therefore, and testify in the Lord, that from now on you do not walk as other Gentiles walk, in the futility of their mind, Having the understanding darkened, being alienated from the life of God through the ignorance that is in them, because of the blindness

of their heart: Who being past feeling have given themselves over unto sensuality, to work all uncleanness with greediness. (Ephesians 5.17-18, KJBT)

Turns from Walking like Gentiles

Paul contrasts the Christian walk of purity with the Gentiles who walked in impurity, without a thought of God. The Gentiles walked in depravity, devoid of truth and anything appropriate. They thought, perceived, processed, and understood life through their sinful nature.

Being "devoid of truth" meant their minds, emotions, and desires were spiritually dark. Paul describes our estrangement from the living God. They were ignorant of any sacred form of spirituality and even calloused to the things of God. Paul expounds on this pervasive spiritual blindness among the lost in 2 Corinthians.

> But even if our gospel is veiled, it is veiled to those who are perishing, whose minds the god of this age has blinded, who do not believe, lest the light of the gospel of the glory of Christ, who is the image of God, should shine on them. (2 Corinthians 4.3-4, NKJV)

The Gentiles given to sensuality were past feelings, meaning they were apathetic toward spiritual things. It was their spiritual mode of operation. They were a sensate culture that marginalized the light of conscience. Carnality and unbridled lust were the order of the day in such a godless culture. Many had broken away from such a lifestyle to walk in a renewed mind. A renewed walk begins as a battle in the mind.

Walking as a New Person

The new man in Christ lives renewing his mind. In other words, because of Christ, his thinking changes from being driven by deceitful lusts and corruption to what is true, righteous, and holy. The mind is the battlefield for a believer's spiritual victory or defeat. Like taking off an old garment, the believer "takes off" the old sinful man and puts on the new person in Christ. The Christian life is set apart unto Christ, as Holy to the Lord, because the believer belongs wholly to the Lord.

> But you have not so learned Christ; If it be that you have heard him, and have been taught by him, as the truth is

in Jesus: That you put off concerning your former self the old man, which is corrupt according to the deceitful lusts; And be renewed in the spirit of your mind; And that you put on the new man, which after God is created in righteousness and true holiness. Therefore, putting away lying and speak every man truth with his neighbor: for we are members one of another.
(Ephesians 5. 22-25, KJBT)

Believers should live right before the Lord because we are indeed members of one another. We stir up one another to what is righteous, pure, and holy. Our responsibility is to live holy, righteously, and godly in this present age. We are equipped and empowered for such a life.

Conclusion

Walking in the steps of Jesus is a worthy walk in line with our calling. How is your walk with the body of Christ? Are you plugged in and connected to God's purpose through the church? He has gifted you with opportunities to be involved in a local fellowship. The Christian life is not a spiritual spectator program of hearing music and sermons. Discipleship is much more. Just like the disciples, it was a hands-on learning experience.

A discipleship challenge might involve seeing how close you can get to Jesus in daily loving devotion. Ask for an awareness of His work in the body of Christ and around you. Surrender yourself to loving what He loved. Jesus loved the church that He gave himself for it. How much do you love what Jesus loved?

Let all bitterness, and wrath, and anger, and quarreling, and evil speaking, be put away from you, with all malice:

And be kind one to another, tenderhearted, forgiving one another, even as God for Christ's sake has forgiven you.
Ephesians 4. 31-32, (KJBT)

Uncommon Kindness

Chapter Ten

Ephesians 4.18-32

Conflict is all around us! Your latest news feed reveals that countries are at war, with rumors of war as growing international fissures deepen. There are internal conflicts within nations, with riots. The streets of America are becoming more and more permeated with violence. Tension and conflicts are pervasive in workplaces. Our children worry about bullying and violence at schools.

Incivility arises at sporting events or on the highways all across the land. Out-of-control emotions spill over quickly because of congested traffic or bad calls at the ballgame. Our culture is driven by the fast life and winning at all costs. It is this me-first mentality that shoves us into endless cycles of conflict. In the maddening hurry, common courtesy is out the window. But this is only the surface of the problem. This problem only reveals the bankruptcy within the soul of many people.

Our children feel the pressure of endless activities, sporting events, homework assignments, and life "without boundaries." The maddening pace is not satisfying. It is more panic-driven and anxious. There is a better way of living.

What describes 21st-century America is also descriptive of the Roman Empire and particularly first-century Ephesus. The Roman Empire neither nurtured inner tranquility nor social harmony. In a social climate riddled with conflict and dissatisfaction, the strong arm of Rome was ready to pounce upon any hint of rebellion. Becoming a Christ-follower in the pagan environment of Ephesus was met with suspicion and a watchful eye.

A vibrant, growing faith in Christ was difficult for anyone immersed in the life and activities of the larger culture. No, their newfound faith in Christ presented believers with a whole new set of conflicts to internalize. Among such "godless" influences of lying, stealing, cheating, crude language and entertainment, greed, sexual impurity, and immorality were all common vices they would struggle with. It was the Gentile way of living. It required a firm commitment to Christ to live faithfully as a first-century Christian.

Uncommon Kindness

Right in the middle of the world's broken mess, the incarnation of God's love infiltrated the ruins. Jesus pitched his tent among the people. The church embodies Christ's love. We are God's mission of uncommon kindness called grace. That's the way God intended it. It is a gathering of grace in an ungracious world! The kind of grace that Paul unpacks is so uncommon that it stands out compared to how the culture views kindness.

It is incarnational kindness, authentic and without pretense. It is on a mission of living God's mercy and love among people. It is intentional kindness. A disciple who follows in the steps of Jesus sees themselves as a conduit of God's grace in the world. We become the good news in the flesh that points to Jesus.

Incarnational

The church lives differently from the culture. People who believe the truth of the Gospel have a lifestyle of truth. They do not make lying a practice. Their words are sacred. Greed and stealing do not govern their actions. They are self-controlled and generous. Likewise, their speech is encouraging and edifying and "minister's grace to the hearers." Therefore, Paul describes a coherent worldview (teaching) and a consistent lifestyle (ethics).

> Therefore putting away lying and speak every man truth with his neighbor: for we are members one of another. Be angry and do not sin, do not let the sun go down upon your wrath: Neither give opportunity to the devil. Let him who stole steal no more: but rather let him labor, working with his hands the thing, which is good, that he may have to give to him who is in need. (Ephesians 4.25-28, KJBT)

How we conduct our lives is more convincing of what we believe than what we say. I had an employer who once said, "People will remember how you made them feel, in how you treat them." These are wise words from a man who understood the power of human behavior. In a corrupt and crooked world, people who believe the Bible is true live truthfully. Truth guides their heart.

Among all the pluralism of Ephesus, the gospel was the ultimate reality of truth lived out. The gospel of truth (1.13) is the word of salvation. Out of respect for Christ and His body, we live truthfully. It is a bond that holds us together as "members of one another." Like the Apostle Paul, our lives are an open book. Deceit has no place in Christ's body or relationships. "One another" is a phrase Paul uses extensively in his letters and comprises the corpus of his Christology.

Self-restraint is another characteristic of the life "in Christ." Christ empowers self-control through the work of the Holy Spirit. Self-mastery is a fruit of the Holy Spirit that flows out of love. It is the yielding of oneself to the Lordship of Christ. It recognizes that anger is a secondary emotion. It is given to Christ and does not harbor anger, bitterness, resentment, and revenge. "Getting even" is characteristic of the kingdoms of this world. The believer yields the wrongs to Christ's righteous judgment. Anger and deception are tools in the working of evil in the world. Satan uses these devices to gain a foothold in our lives and ruin the testimony of the gospel in the world.

A positive work ethic also characterizes the life of faith. Gratitude and generosity are poignant anecdotes for greed. The grace-gathered church is wild with unbridled generosity toward one another. The unique ministry of the early church is their care for one another's needs. Deacons served in the ministry to widows, orphans, and those in need. It is unique in a self-absorbed culture where self-gratification is the highest motivation.

The Words We Speak

The gathering of the faithful speaks differently. Interestingly, we call this self-expression. We self-express with words. So does God! Our words flow from the depths of our hearts and who we are. Paul admonished the believers not to fall into the crude self-expressions that characterized the Ephesian culture but to minister grace to the hearers.

> Let no corrupt communication proceed out of your mouth, but rather that which is good to the use of edifying, that it may minister grace unto the hearers. And do not grieve the Holy Spirit of God, by whom you are sealed unto the day of redemption.
> (Ephesians 4. 29-30, KJBT)

Our words, attitudes, motivations, and desires are to be shaped by the character of Christ. Gracious words were encouraged by the wisest of Jewish and Greek teachers. A grace-gathered church should especially exemplify grace-filled words.

Paul admonishes the Ephesians against corrupt words (unwholesome or filthy *sapros*). It is colorful and descriptive of what is putrid or rotten. Perhaps Paul had in mind the smells of the *agora* (marketplace). Smelly rotten fruit or rancid fish might fill the air. The believer's language should not be repulsive, harsh, or critical. Words build up and affirm others in a most holy faith. I imagine weary believers gathering in house churches with hope-filled, encouraging words, gracious greetings, and blessing Christ's name in worship. What an encouraging and healthy environment of love.

Lived Out in Relationships

The gathered fellowship of believers is a grace-filled community of love that builds up. A healthy church cultivates such an environment. Paul provides specific insight into what such a community looks like.

> Let all bitterness, and wrath, and anger, and quarreling, and evil speaking, be put away from you, with all malice: And be kind one to another, tenderhearted, forgiving one another, even as God for Christ's sake has forgiven you. (Ephesians 4. 31-32, KJBT)

Bitterness is a bitter pool of resentment that leads to a seething boil within that leads to an emotional expression that desires to punish. It is a toxic pool that leads to quarreling and slanderous talking about others and a malicious ill-will that is abusive. Such forms of self-expression create and nurture an environment of division, strife, contention, and hurt feelings within the family.

People become disillusioned with the most holy faith and the church. The person of the Holy Spirit is deeply grieved, and Satan gains a foothold and certain victory. The ancient wisdom of Proverbs 15.1 reminds us that a soft answer turns away wrath, but harsh words stir up anger.

Positively, uncommon and deliberate kindness characterizes the church. Kindness is disarming, making its way toward reconciliation, drawing from the deeper wells of empathy and compassion. It seeks understanding and building trust. What does this uncommon kindness look like? These two passages provide us with the relational dynamics for harmony. How do you get to a positive place in relationships?

Intentional Kindness

Relinquish Retaliation

We all deal with being wronged by others, either by hurtful words or actions. Even so, we are to be kind to one another. Kindness is an issue of your character. It is the clothing of the believer. Respect and courtesy go a long way in relationships. Being in Christ and empowered by the Holy Spirit, we can relinquish retaliation and replace it with uncommon kindness.

We either nurture grievances that root down in bitterness or plant kindness. See to it that no one comes short of the grace of God; that no root of bitterness springing up causes trouble, and by it may be defiled (cf. Hebrews 12.15). This ethic characterized the early church. They were indeed a grace-gathering that did not repay evil for evil but lived to bless others by overcoming with good. (cf. 1 Peter 3.9, Romans 12.21).

Conflict or Opportunity

Recognize that relational conflicts often reflect internal conflicts within us. It could be "unmet needs" or blocked goals that fuel the struggle. In our swirling inward turmoils, we give "knee-jerk" responses that only deepen and widen relational conflicts.

As a believer, you can exhibit emotional control through the Lordship of Christ. Yield your emotions to Christ in prayer. As your high priest,

Jesus understands what you feel. Trust your feelings to His Lordship. Negative emotions drain our motivation and keep us spiritually weak and weary. Christ will renew our strength.

Align your mind with truth and seek God's wisdom and strength through the power of the Holy Spirit. To live in the freedom of Christ requires bringing every thought to obedience to the truth of Scripture and Christ into our words and deeds.

Confession of sin breaks the strongholds in our thinking and behavior that feed the conflict. By recognizing and turning from negative thoughts and behavior patterns, we can bring conflicting emotions under the control of Christ's Lordship. Emotional healing is possible, and this is the beginning point. How do we handle conflict? Peaceably! Humility, wisdom, and reasonableness are essential qualities for what Jesus called the peacemakers.

Seek Understanding

Paul calls the grace-gathering people to "tender-heartedness." It leans more into empathy and love that seeks understanding. It does not necessarily mean *agreement* with someone, as much as understanding the "why" behind the tension. Our purest motivation is not being "right" but living out Christ's love. Paul reminded the Ephesians that they should not keep the conflict stirred up through outbursts, anger, quarreling, slander, and malice. The spirit that seeks understanding keeps the heart from harshness, hardness, and bitterness. It is possible to be gracious and grace-filled in an environment of tension.

Release through Forgiveness

Jesus knew that in the relational world, there were conflicts and tension. Because of the inherent sinful nature, it just stands to reason that misunderstandings and conflicts arise. Remember how he taught His disciples to pray. God is our heavenly Father–the most holy and intimate. His fatherly domain is his kingdom–both present and coming. He has a will on earth like he does in heaven. The Father provides and nourishes His children with daily bread and forgiveness. Jesus recognized that we would not only need forgiveness, but we would need to extend forgiveness in relationships. Conflicts are opportunities for heaven's will on earth.

Forgiveness is at the core of the Christian gospel. We can accept God's forgiveness and thus forgive ourselves for past sins and forgive the offense of others. Forgiveness is what the cross is all about. The cross of Christ is the one climatic act of human history, where heaven's glory meets man in his vilest shame in the sacrifice of love. God's deep mercies and forgiveness extend at the cross. It is the place where life can start over and begin anew. It is a life-changer. It changes everything within us and for us, for now and eternity!

We are empowered to release others of past wrongs through forgiveness. It is a virtue. Forgiveness on a human level may or may not involve reconciliation. Reconciliation is impossible in some cases, especially where a person is deceased.

A toxic relationship is often not easily mended, and separation is necessary. It would be unwise and unsafe, such as in the case of domestic abuse or violence. Forgiveness granted does not negate the moral and sometimes legal consequences of certain injustices. A person's life can move forward, and a sense of inner peace is experienced through forgiveness, even though the social aspects of the relationship are severed.

Forgiveness allows one to release the pain and hurt and move forward with living. Instead of hanging onto the emotional hurts of offenses, the believer follows the heart of the Savior and releases the grudge. Those who practice forgiveness experience release from Satan's stronghold and bitter roots.

The healthy church is grace-filled. The *Amazing Grace* we sing about lives in relationships. The church is a conduit of grace. It means we understand the depth of grace that prompts the Father's forgiveness of us. It displays the power of God's forgiveness and makes the gospel believable to the world.

Missional Kindness

Uncommon kindness means our heart has not become embittered in recovering from life's hurts. The grace-gathered community then is on a mission of God's merciful kindness. The act of forgiveness is simply imitating a family trait—the grace of the Heavenly Father. It is the mission of the grace gathering in a broken world.

> Therefore, be imitators of God, as dear children; And walk in love, as Christ also has loved us, and has given himself for us an offering and a sacrifice to God for a sweet-smelling savor.   (Ephesians 5.1-2, KJBT)

God is love! Believers imitate their Heavenly Father's love through forgiveness and loving others. Kingdom people follow hard after God to live as He lives. The kingdom culture aligns itself in the light of God's nature. Deliberate kindness is part of her mission in a broken world. God's nature is moral light, and His children reflect God's light in a dark world.

Conclusion

God's new community is a grace gathering. It is a safe place for those dealing with hurts, hang-ups, and heartaches. It is a place where sinners find forgiveness, hope, and healing. It is truly a community that is different from anything in the world. It is built upon grace and marked by kindness.

It is God's kindness lived out like Jesus' incarnation, intentionally as God's mission in the broken world. As an imitator of God, we put on display that God so loved the world He gave His one and only Son so that whosoever believes in Jesus has eternal life. Jesus saved us in our broken messes. He will save whoever calls upon His name.

The Subtle Slide into Sense-Driven Living

Chapter Eleven

Ephesians 5.3-16

"Oh, be careful little eyes what you see, there's a Father up above, Who is looking down with love, Oh be careful little eyes what you see." In an age of instant imagery on computers, televisions, and phones, we are prone to suspend our thinking. We become numbed by mindless entertainment. It is easily accessible and addictive. The lyrics to this old children's song are never more relevant. They remind us to guard our senses (see, hear, touch, taste, smell). We relate to the world through sense. That's how we understand and experience the world around us.

We become subconsciously influenced by the images we see, the lyrics we hear, the taste buds we develop, and the things within our grasp. These become the air of life and what we breathe in deeply. What shapes our lives can subtly seduce us into destructive pursuits that derail us morally. But usually, before our lives are overturned and messy, there are deep spiritual fissures left unchecked. In this lesson, Paul exposes the dark appeal of the world. The pervasive spiritual darkness subtly overtakes our hearts and our devotion to Christ. It's like an attraction of dark clouds of an approaching storm.

Lurking underneath the world's pursuits, habits, and motivations is the internal appeal of the sinful nature within us. It is what Paul calls the world, the fleshly appetites, influenced by the devils' diabolical rebellion against God. Ephesians 2.2 states that we find its appeal because it draws upon the base carnal desires of what Paul calls the old man, dead in trespasses of sin.

> Who were dead in trespasses and sins, in which you once walked according to the course of this world, according to the prince of the power of the air, the spirit who now works in the sons of disobedience, among

> whom also we all once conducted ourselves in the lusts of our flesh, fulfilling the desires of the flesh and of the mind, and were by nature children of wrath, just as the others. (Ephesians 2.1-3, KJBT)

We find fleshly things appealing because our inherent nature is sinful. Without a sin-nature, it really wouldn't be a temptation. Without the regenerating work of the Holy Spirit, people live in a conscious estrangement from the Creator. The cultural drive is the senses. As theologian and cultural scholar Harold Brown would refer to it–the "sensate culture." Cultures morally digress in personal virtue and ethics when they lean into pleasing the senses. Ephesus had seemingly mastered the art. They were a sense-driven culture.

Sacred vs. Sensual

Paul challenged the Ephesian believers, who were readily seated in the middle of Ephesian sensuality, to be imitators of God. (Ephesians 5.1-2) Said another way, for believers today in the middle of a sense-driven culture and a broader secular vision, our challenge is that we must lean into the sacred. Christians of all ages are to be holy as God is holy.

The believer's imitation of the Father includes a consecrated lifestyle to God and love toward others. A godly or theocentric lifestyle reflects the Holy nature of our Father. It is a family trait! It walks in the steps of Christ with a desire to please the Father.

> Therefore, be imitators of God, as dear children; And walk in love, as Christ also has loved us, and has given himself for us an offering and a sacrifice to God for a sweet-smelling savor. But sexual immorality, and all uncleanness, or covetousness, let in not once be named among you, as becomes saints; (Ephesians 5.1-3, KJBT)

Let's look at how believers are to be imitators of God.

Imitation is a form of flattery. Better said, it is a way of magnifying our Father. The believer displays the family trait of holiness as His child in the world. In chapter 4, Paul shows how believers should interact with others. In chapter 5, Paul addresses the believer's challenge to live pure in an impure world. The church is to live holy and in the wholeness of Christ. Let us now explore the dangers of a sense-driven life.

Sense-Driven Culture

Paul lists three characteristics of a people given over to live for what they can see, touch, feel, or taste. Given fleshly pleasure rather than the pleasure of God, self-fulfillment motivates choices, attitudes, and behaviors.

Religious paganism, crude entertainment, and the exploitation of people characterized the city. Greek and Roman culture celebrated and idolized the human body. Statues and religious icons of the day displayed the human body, and the Greek games played in the nude. Culture and life gravitated naturally to the sensual and the appetites of the flesh.

The Roman games eventually were marked by horrid violence in the Colosseum. A whole trail of bloodshed of the Christian martyrs died in the area as a spectacle for public entertainment. Such sadistic impulses of moral bankruptcy and spiritual darkness revealed the deep fractures of the eroding foundations. The Roman Empire would eventually collapse due to the moral decline of the population and culture. It is a sobering lesson in human history. As the moral foundations weaken, the civil structures will eventually collapse. It is inevitable.

Temple prostitution (male and female) was "normal" in the city life. It was a spiritual and cultural practice. The Roman fast life was an accepted part of life. A sensate culture moves fast, indulging the next sensual pleasure. It is never satisfied. It just deepens in depravity. Jewish families devoted to the Torah (law) and converts to Christ would have struggled with such an environment.

Sensual Appetites over Sacred Devotion

So, what characterized the sensual life of the Roman Empire was fornication *porneia*. It is the word we understand as pornography and specifically illicit sexual activity outside of marriage, most commonly practiced among the Greeks. The implications and meaning of the word were much broader. It involved uncleanness in the internal moral sense of lustful motives and filthy living. It was greedy and given to wanton desires.

Those in lifestyles given to sensual pleasures are never fully satisfied because the flesh cannot produce spiritual satisfaction. Our culture has been in a steady moral decline since the sexual revolution of the 1960s. We are experiencing the devastating results of sexual abuse and broken families. A rising drug culture fuels crime and violence. Loosening self-restraint and common civility leads to moral collapse. Without a moral underpinning, social collapse is inevitable. The message of the Gospel is the only hope for a sensate culture.

De-Sacralized Use of Words

Conversations centered around shameful practices, sexual innuendo, and immorality are not even to be mentioned among God's children. Pornography, uncleanness, and greed were characteristic of idolaters in spiritual darkness, not the children of light. Spoken words reveal the depth of what's in the heart. Paul reminds believers that the judgment of God is coming upon the wicked practices of disobedience in spiritual darkness.

> Neither filthiness, nor foolish talking, nor jesting, which are not fitting: but rather giving of thanks. For this you know that no sexually immoral person, nor unclean person, nor covetous man, who is an idolater, has any inheritance in the kingdom of Christ and of God. Let no man deceive you with empty words: for because of these things the wrath of God is coming upon the children of disobedience.　　　(Ephesians 5. 5-7 KJBT)

Paul characterizes the nature of the language used in flesh-driven or sense-oriented culture. Filthy, base, or shameful talk is ordinary in a sensate culture. Using language that is dishonoring, coarse jesting as scurrile, and offensive remarks discredits one's witness of Christ.

The doctrine of grace is not to be abused because God does not treat man's sin lightly. Judgment awaits the children of disobedience. The grace-gathered community should not fall for the deceptive words of slick preachers or cultural influencers who soft-pedal the importance of personal purity as prudish. As the larger culture "buys into" and markets suggestive ideas or trends, it is usually not good news for your soul or spiritual health, regardless of the freedom that it promises.

The gnostics with (lawless) antinomian tendencies asserted that the actions of the body did not affect the spirit. These gnostics would see no need for separating from immoral world practices. Paul's admonition to imitate the heavenly Father echoes the wisdom literature: *Guard your heart with all diligence, for out of it flows the issues of life.* Proverbs 4.23

Shaped by the Seen

There is a subtle danger of temporal images and living for the moment rather than for what is unseen and eternal. Paul gives a warning to those given to the habitual lifestyle of idolatry.

Image-Driven

The Ten Commandments warned God's children not to make graven images and have other gods. The human hands that make the idols become the object of affection and worship. Covenant children are different. They exclusively worship Yahweh in a covenant relationship. We promote, fixate on, and become like what we idolize. The heart has a natural propensity to worship idols. It takes no prompting!

Our modern idols are not golden calves but more sophisticated. Images of success, materialism, and pleasure consume our thinking. Money and riches, prestige and power are alluring. Americans value rugged individualism, self-expression, and personal freedom. We can even idolize our morality, religious expression, or version of ministry over wholehearted devotion to Christ. The pull of idolatry is subtle.

With ease, we center our lives around our feelings, thoughts, aspirations, goals, hurts and heartaches, successes and glory. We become obsessed and blinded to it and by it. Said another way, we cannot rightly see our worth when we feel the tug and pressures of a sensate culture trying to shape that image for us.

Self-absorbed lives focus on the material, and ingratitude seizes the soul with a gripping paralysis. There has never been a time in human history that we can live out self-absorption more fully.

You can take endless pictures of yourself. It is the lure of the camera in our hands. Our self-expressions are the subtle seduction of the heart that makes us the center of living. We can see our material selves reflected in the mirror. Narcissism is the buzzword of the day. It's subtle, you see, and our souls become emptier and dissatisfied. What if God were to take a picture of our soul? What would we see in the depths of our hearts?

Whatever we fix our gaze upon becomes the treasure of the heart. The words we speak reveal the depth of the heart's treasure. Image-driven pursuits ultimately leave us feeling empty inside. God has created us for more than for the superficial stuff that defines us. God created us for intimacy with our Father.

Word-Oriented Living

Our post-modern era has desacralized the use of words. In the spirit of the age, subjective interpretation outweighs an objective literal meaning. Feelings carry more weight.

When God chose to reveal himself, how did he do it? God's self-revelation at creation was not by image but by His *word*. God speaks and creates out of nothing and declares it good. There is an aesthetic beauty recognized and moral goodness that reflects His nature in creation and His word.

Gratitude is the recognition and appreciation of the good things before our eyes as good. Gratitude then is marked by thanksgiving *eucharisteo* for the blessing of good things. Appreciation for what God does yields adoring worship for Who He is, with nothing less than our life.

Worship is the blessing of the goodness of God. Worship God for who He is! Tune your heart with gratitude by recognizing and thanking him for what He does. William Temple said, *"To worship is to quicken the conscience by the holiness of God, to feed the mind with the truth of God, to purge the imagination with the beauty of God, to open the heart to the love of God and to devote the will to the purpose of God."* We eventually become like what we worship.

Gratitude aligns our hearts with the good and keeps our senses in check. Incorporating intentional gratitude is like an antidote for the ailing heart prone to being sidetracked by empty pursuits. Thanksgiving then leans into the value of the sacred. It is the recognition that every perfect gift comes from the Father of light. It points to something outside ourselves with intrinsic value and worth–

God. Giving thanks is then the proper use of words recognizing the sacred.

The words we speak are a great place to start. Hear yourself give thanks. It helps raise your sights much higher than what glitters down here. Ingratitude robs the soul until the spiritual house is left abandoned of anything meaningful in life!

Lives for the Moment

The third spiritual slide is the pursuit of the experience of the moment. The sight of eternal purpose gets lost in the moment. It is easy to be passive when it comes to spiritual matters. Paul contrasts a life of darkness, characterized by spiritual and moral ignorance, with light. Light is the spiritual and moral illumination for a spiritually healthy and satisfying life.

A sense-driven culture slips into despair while the grace-gathered community stands in hope. We are joint partakers with the King of Heaven and possess eternal riches–one day gloriously unveiled. The children of light will fully experience their inheritance.

> Therefore, do not be partakers with them. For once you were darkness, but now you are light in the Lord: walk as children of light: (For the fruit of the Spirit is in all goodness and righteousness and truth) Determine what is acceptable unto the Lord. And have no fellowship with the unfruitful works of darkness, but rather expose them. For it is a shame even to speak of those things which are done by them in secret. But all things that are exposed are made clear by the light: for what exposes is light. (Ephesians 5.8-13, KJBT)

Paul interweaves His understanding of life in the Holy Spirit's empowerment related to goodness, righteousness, and truth. The pursuit of the believer is like that of Christ. His meat and drink were to do the will of the Father. The believer is pleased to live for the Father's will. So, with great determination, the believer seeks to discern the will of the Lord.

Goodness is the uprightness of heart and life that would include kindness. It recognizes that God is the source of goodness. It flows from

Him. Believers must live in righteousness. Righteousness is a life of integrity and virtue. It thinks rightly about God and clearly about oneself. Upright living and freedom from falsehood and deceit characterize such a life. It is in perfect harmony with the God of truth.

The motivation of the follower of Christ is discerning what is acceptable to His pleasure and exposing or bringing to light the works of darkness done in secret. It pre-judges the sin and brings to light what is darkness. Children of light are not partakers of such darkness. What is exposed by the light reveals sin and calls for confession of sin, repentance (turning from sin), and restoration to fellowship with God.

Remember what Paul previously reminded the Ephesian believers, that they were members of one another. Christian love compels the fellowship to seek the restoration of an erring brother or sister.

Slumbers in Darkness

Paul exposes a fourth spiritual danger in the slide to sensuality. A careless spiritual slumber rocks the believers to sleep. This rich theological truth comes in the form of a hymn.

Paul's letters are replete with prayers and praise. Proper theology always leads to heartfelt doxology. Most scholars agree that a portion of verse 14 is a Christian hymn. Recipients would understand the lyrical element of the text. Scholars suggest that the source material is Isaiah 26.19.

> Your dead shall live; Together with my dead body they shall arise. Awake and sing, you who dwell in dust; For your dew is like the dew of herbs, And the earth shall cast out the dead. (NKJV)

The Ephesians were encouraged to arise from the spiritual lethargy of pagan surroundings, anchoring in the powerful good news of the resurrection of Christ and shining the light of the gospel among all people. This section speaks almost like a reveille, a call to alertness.

> Therefore, he said, Awake you who sleep, and arise from the dead, and Christ shall give you light. See then that you walk looking around, not as fools, but as wise, making the best use of the time because the days are

> evil. Therefore, do not be unwise, but understand what
> the will of the Lord is.   (Ephesians 5.14-17, KJBT)

Spiritual darkness surrounding you can lead you to a place of complacency and apathy. We are to be awakened and aroused from a pervasive spiritual darkness. Paul's admonition is urgent. It is not only to be awakened from spiritual carelessness but also to arise out of the sin that quickly overtakes our lives.

The Gentile mind was captivated by ignorance and ungodliness. Spiritual indifference is crippling and dangerous. Just as Jesus' resurrection from the grave, we rise to walk in the new life of Christ. We arise from the deadness of sin to life in God.

Remember we were dead in trespasses and sin (2.4-5) and walked in the futility of mind with our understanding darkened, ignorant and alienated, blind, past feeling, given to lewdness and uncleanness (4.17-19). The believer must stand up and walk in step with eternity. *"See then that you walk circumspectly, not as fools but as wise, redeeming the time, because the days are evil."* (Ephesians 5.16)

The passionate walk for the Lord walks carefully and discerningly by taking heed of their spiritual state. He walks circumspectly, with great diligence. They focus on Christ and follow His steps. It is a walk of practical wisdom–a wise walk with eternity in view. It rejects living for the moment's sinful pleasure.

Time presupposes forward movement and the implication of change. For such a time as this, we should pursue meaningful living. Seriously examine and weigh our priorities and use of time with the godly wisdom of Scripture.

Conclusion

Time keeps moving forward, and we can't get it back, but we can redeem it by making every moment count for eternity. The days quickly slip into eternity and to the eternal God, who is immutable. All things in time will return to Him where He rightly stands as judge of the living and the dead.

The lateness of the hour and darkness of the day should compel us to watch and pray. Awake from the spiritual slumber without passion to a devoted commitment to Christ. Time grows shorter! Eternity looms long! Christ stands at the door to awaken those asleep. Can you hear Him knocking? He is pleading for fellowship with His church. Only you can open that door. How long will you slumber? Awake O Sleeper!

Do not love the world,
neither the things that are in the world.
If any man loves the world,
the love of the Father is not in him.
For all that is in the world,
the lust of the flesh,
and the lust of the eyes,
and the pride of life,
is not of the Father,
but is of the world.
And the world passes away,
and the lust of it:
but he who does
the will of God abides forever.
(I John 2.15-17, KJBT)

The Incredible Life in the Spirit

Chapter Twelve

Ephesians 5.17-21

What are the controlling impulses of your life?

The Apostle to the Gentiles alludes to a common cultural practice–wild parties. Paul reminded the followers of Christ that the days were indeed evil. Drunkenness often accompanied the deep-seated pursuit of pleasure by deadening the internal restraint of self-control. Someone under the controlling influence of intoxicating drink or "spirits" obviously walks like someone under the influence. Paul says it leads to "riotous living" or "debauchery." Paul most probably had in mind the lewd activities associated with temple goddess worship.

Upon entering the port city of Ephesus, a 50-foot statue of Domitian was an intimidating reminder of Roman rule and the emperor as the "god of all gods". As mentioned earlier, the city was a religious center hosting gods and goddesses for worship. The temple of Artemis was one of fourteen pagan temples in the city. The worship of Artemis (Roman Diana) was the Greek goddess of hunting, forests, fertility, and childbirth. The routines of daily life, such as commerce and banking, happened at the temple.

The massive temple of Artemis was one of the seven wonders of the ancient world. This magnificent temple with male and female temple prostitutes celebrated the goddess. Festive musical processions with her statues lingered into the night. Wild parties and lascivious dances were performed in her honor, culminating in drunken orgies.[1]

> And do not be drunk with wine, which leads to riotous living; but be filled with the Spirit; Speaking to

---

[1] See Endnote link, Joseph Stowell, Ephesus: The Seven Churches of Revelation, Our DailyBread.

> yourselves in psalms and hymns and spiritual songs, singing and making melody in your heart to the Lord; Giving thanks always for all things unto God and the Father in the name of our Lord Jesus Christ; (Ephesians 5.17-19, KJBT)

Dionysius is the cult of fruit and winemaking, partying, and pleasure. The symbol of the cult of Dionysus was the vine. He was the patron god of stage, entertainment, and theater. Drunkenness, insanity, and religious ecstasy was the way to connect with the gods. The orgiastic cult was strongly dualistic. They believed that a corrupt body restrained the soul.[2] In our day and time, Dionysus might be the object of worship for many spring breakers.

In stark contrast, the grace-gathering people lived under the controlling influence of the Holy Spirit. The Christian finds his joy in the pleasure of God. It draws deeply from the internal well of the Holy Spirit. The Christian life is more than a system of ethics or philosophy of living. It is the life of Christ lived through the believer. The world lives for what pleases the senses, whereas the Christian life operates in the fullness of the Spirit. Paul said so much to the Corinthians believers that they were indeed the new temple of God.

> Flee sexual immorality. Every sin that a man does is outside the body, but he who commits sexual immorality sins against his own body. Or do you not know that your body is the temple of the Holy Spirit *who is* in you, whom you have from God, and you are not your own? For you were bought at a price; therefore, glorify God in your body and in your spirit, which are God's.
> (1 Corinthians 6.18-20, NKJV)

The Jewish readers would also understand very well the temple motif. God's Holy presence would fill the temple (being made by men's hands) with His glory. Johannine scholars point out that Jesus presented himself as the new temple of God, in contrast to the corrupt temple of his day. In Christ's incarnation, God pitched a new tent where

---

[2] See James Feffers, The Greco-Roman World of the New Testament Era, Exploring the Background of Early Christianity, IVP, Academic, Downers Grove.

the fullness of His presence abode–the person of Jesus Christ. (cf. John 1.14)

Jesus told Nicodemus that kingdom entrance required a birth from above by the Spirit. The inauguration of Jesus' ministry involved turning water into wine at Cana of Galilee. His ministry would be a cause of great joy. Jesus described the coming of the Holy Spirit as rivers of living water.

> On the last day, that great *day* of the feast, Jesus stood and cried out, saying, "If anyone thirsts, let him come to Me and drink. He who believes in Me, as the Scripture has said, out of his heart will flow rivers of living water.
> (John 7.37-38, NKJV)

The very presence of Jesus was light and the life of men. It was the fullness of life for believers. Paul expands it that now the believer is the temple of God, where the Holy Spirit abides and dwells. The very life of God Himself is the work of the Holy Spirit. Paul unpacks this concept in the book of Ephesus and the larger corpus of his epistles.

The Function of the Holy Spirit

The life of the Holy Spirit within us bears spiritual fruit. Paul describes the virtues of goodness, truth, and righteousness. These are the building blocks for healthy relationships. These virtues are expressed in the fruit of the Spirit: love, joy, peace, long-suffering, patience, etc. It works out in the gathering of God's people through singing, psalms, hymns, and spiritual songs, and also with a heart of deep gratitude lives out in thanksgiving. At this juncture, it is at least helpful to recall what Paul has taught the Ephesian believers about the Holy Spirit and draw from the larger corpus of Paul.

Paul reminds us of the work of the Holy Spirit. He gives wisdom, revelation, and knowledge of Christ (1.17). The believer comes into a relationship with God through preaching the gospel and the conviction of the Holy Spirit, who draws people to hear, believe, and receive through receiving Christ's work of salvation. Paul reminds us that this was the gospel message preached by the holy apostles and prophets through the Holy Spirit by which Gentiles were made partakers also. (cf. Ephesians 3.4-7)

> "The word is near you, in your mouth and in your heart" (that is, the word of faith which we preach): that if you confess with your mouth the Lord Jesus and believe in your heart that God has raised Him from the dead, you will be saved. For with the heart one believes unto righteousness, and with the mouth confession is made unto salvation. (Romans 10.8-10, NKJV)

The Holy Spirit imparts new life to those once estranged from God in their spiritual deadness (2.5-7). It is the marvelous work of grace by which the believer's salvation is by grace through faith. Regeneration is the work of the Holy Spirit through Christ's mercy (cf. Titus 3.5). The renewal of the Spirit renders the believer justified or declared righteous before God.

As discussed in previous chapters, the Holy Spirit's presence was a deposit that guarantees that God's redemptive work is complete. The Holy Spirit indwells believers who are the new temple of God fitted together in the world (2.17-18). The Holy Spirit baptizes believers into the body of Christ. Having the Holy Spirit means belonging to Jesus (cf. Romans 8.9). The Holy Spirit is personal. He leads and works as the believer's helper.

He is the sword of the Spirit, who works through the power of God's word (6.17). He is the Spirit of truth. He works as an intercessor on the believer's behalf with access to the Father (2.17-18). The Holy Spirit's sealing is God's guarantee upon believers that He claims us as His own by placing His official seal upon us. Believers are empowered to be led and walk in the Spirit of God. This new life is one of godliness and obedience. Disobedience then is personally grievous to the Holy Spirit (4.30).

The Holy Spirit is operative in regeneration, sanctification, baptizing, indwelling, and sealing the believer. His work brings glory to Christ (John 16.14) and enables believers to glorify God. The Holy Spirit conforms believers to the image of Christ. Paul describes a continual work of the Holy Spirit in this passage in Ephesians 5.17. He describes the filling of the Holy Spirit as a continual, ongoing, daily process. It is not a one-time work of the Holy Spirit. How does this practically happen in the believer's life? What characterizes one filled with the Holy Spirit?

Be Being Filled

Often, people think they would be further along in their Christian walk if circumstances were better. Life's troubles can become like a heavy weight that feels suffocating. A better environment, health, friends, money, or perhaps a change in scenery might give us some life in our breath. Unfortunately, the Christian life feels more of an obligation than anything incredible. An adventurous journey into God's joy seems distant trying to envision the next step. I am sure it did for Paul as he penned this letter under house arrest.

Many settle that the best life muddles along. God wants us to experience His life. He desires more than a life of ease and comfort, free from conflicts and trouble. He wants the infusion of His presence. As the Psalmist declared, "In His presence, there is fullness of joy." God provides strength for today's journey through the Spirit. Life in the Spirit means God fully invests in our life's journey. He not only walks with us but strengthens our steps. His work exceeds what we can ask or think.

The Ephesian believers were in the middle of a culture that was not cheering on godliness and holy living. They needed inward strength much greater than the pressures surrounding them. Paul pointed them to the deep joy that was greater than the pleasures that Ephesus offered. It was an overcoming strength greater than fleshly temptations, rejection, hostility, persecution, and even imprison- ment. How could they live in a victory over the world, the flesh, and the devil? They simply lived in the greater joy of the Holy Spirit. It was sustaining and strengthening. It is the incredible life in the Spirit.

Controlling Influence

"Being filled with the Holy Spirit" is a continual work. It is not a second work of God's grace as sometimes taught, but rather the daily work of the life of God operating in the believer. It is literally to "be-being" filled with the Spirit. It is dynamic and daily.

Walking in the fullness of the power of the Holy Spirit does not put one "out of control" as in some sort of religious ecstasy characterized by the worship of the gods. The Spirit enables self-mastery for virtuous living and a victory over the flesh.

Consider four ways this works out. Being filled does not require a not self-emptying of sorts. It involves yielding yourself to the controlling influence of the Spirit. Thinking God's thoughts, as revealed in His word, the emotions aligned with His desires and pleasures, and the will yielded in obedience to His life describes submission. The grace-gathered community lives out the fullness of the Holy Spirit. Worship is not stale and lifeless but dynamic and vibrant in His joy! Here is what a spirit-filled church looks like.

Worshipful Singing

Joyful singing characterizes the church. It is more than an ability to sing. Worship is the heart boiling over in the enjoyment of God. It is a melody within the heart. It reflects hearts so captivated by Christ that it overflows with such satisfying joy in the pleasure of God. Hymn singing, praise, dedication, and devotions are spoken and sung in honor of Jesus and to glorify God through His Spirit.

The tone, tenor, and truth of Scripture shape the music and meter. It involves plucking strings or sacred songs accompanied by music. The Holy Spirit directs and empowers the worship endeavor.

Feel Grateful and Live Thankful

The grace-gathered community finds complete satisfaction and joy in Christ. It is Christ-centered and rejoices in Christ. Nowhere do we find, give your complaints to the Lord. They would "give thanks for everything to God the Father in the name of our Lord Jesus Christ." (Ephesians 5.20, KJBT)

Discontentment, manipulation, and complaining are indicators of being under the control of circumstances. It is characteristic of a life without faith. When reducing the goodness of God to how life is going, we tend to equate our faith with the circumstances. If circumstances are not good, is God still good? That's a question to ponder. Complaining is a reflection of our view of God.

The children of Israel complained and murmured, arousing God's anger against them (Numbers 11.1). The purest gift of service flows from a grateful heart.

> Do all things without complaining and disputing, that you may become blameless and harmless, children of God without fault in the midst of a crooked and perverse generation, among whom you shine as lights in the world, holding fast the word of life, so that I may rejoice in the day of Christ that I have not run in vain or labored in vain. (Philippians 2.14-16, NKJV)

The characteristic of the grace-gathered community is thanksgiving with adoration and gratitude of God. Our celebration is God! Gratitude chooses to approach life as an opportunity to celebrate God.

Submits to One Another

The body life of the early church is antithetical to how the world systems operate. Humility was the attitude and mutual submission among one another, creating a thriving environment that was not self-seeking, but Spirit led. Christians were simply different from the world. They submitted to one another out of reverence for Christ. (cf. Ephesians 5.21).

The idea of submission is an alignment. It is a military term meaning to be under the authority of another. So, the control of the Holy Spirit aligns our hearts under Christ's Lordship and lives in humility toward one another. Jesus was our example.

Jesus was co-eternal, co-existent, and co-equal with the Father. He was equal in being and essence as the second person of the Trinity. However, in the practical economy of the Trinity, Jesus prayed in the garden and submitted to the will of His Father. Jesus aligned Himself under the will of His Father. He humbled himself and became obedient unto death.

Ministry to the needs of other believers in the body of Christ is the believer's joyful privilege. We are fellow members. Life in the Spirit means we are becoming more aware of other needs. We are called outside ourselves in ministry to one another. I am amazed how my needs lessen when I focus on Christ and ministry to others. Ministry is one reminder that the world does not revolve around us.

The Fruit of the Holy Spirit

Conforms to Christ

Just because we are new creations in Christ does not mean our sinful nature is gone. The power of sin's grip on us is gone–broken! We can live victorious over it because of the Holy Spirit. Don't let sin reign or be on the throne of your life. Sin is not to have the kingly reign in our personal lives or the life of the gathering. Jesus is the King of the Kingdom, so the believer (once enslaved by sin) is now empowered to live righteously. Paul unpacks this in Roman 6 in greater detail.

The filling of the Holy Spirit conforms us to the image of Christ so that we may glorify God. Again, this happens as the believer yields his mind to the Spirit of truth, his passions and emotions fulfilled through the Spirit, and willful choices in obedience to the will and purposes of God. Fleshly strongholds crumble as the mind of Christ reigns in the surrendered life.

> For though we walk in the flesh, we do not war according to the flesh. For the weapons of our warfare *are* not carnal but mighty in God for pulling down strongholds, casting down arguments and every high thing that exalts itself against the knowledge of God, bringing every thought into captivity to the obedience of Christ, and being ready to punish all disobedience when your obedience is fulfilled.
> (2 Corinthians 10.3-6, NKJV)

The believer is empowered to change his thought life to (whatever is pure, right, honorable, and holy). An alignment of our thinking with the mind of Christ. There is a glorious renewal in the spirit of his mind (4.23). Conformity to Christ happens by turning from the world or sin-dominated thinking, transformed by renewing the mind. (Romans 12.2) The filling of the Holy Spirit means that God gains more control over our lives, not that we get more of God.

Mind Shaped by Truth

Jesus said you shall know the truth–the truth shall set you free (cf. John 8.32). Replacing flesh-oriented thinking habits breaks the cycles of defeat. The spiritual battle is primarily in the mind. Thinking God's thoughts are life-changing. Shaping our desires and passions to truth liberates us from the bondage, misery, and cycles of defeat.

Daily reading, hearing, and meditating on biblical principles helps replace the lies of our self-talk with God's reality. We love God with all our minds, soul, and strength. An integral part of being "set apart" unto Christ as His holy people involves how we think about ourselves and God.

As the believer yields his thinking to truth, negative emotions diminish, and they release us from their grip. When we replace the lies with God's truth over time, our feelings will eventually conform to our new identity in Christ. The Holy Spirit empowers us with His love, joy, and peace. What surrounds you cannot match the power within you through the Holy Spirit. The incredible work of the Holy Spirit is reality from God's perspective.

Empowered Walk of Obedience

Paul finally reminds the believers in Rome that as they walk in the Spirit, they will not fulfill the lusts of the flesh. The spirit-filled walking as Christ walked in the world. Jesus lived for the will of the Father. The believer must walk in faithful obedience. The Holy Spirit empowers faithfulness in an obedient walk in the Lord.

Produces Spiritual Fruit

What does the Holy Spirit produce? What are the virtues at work in the incredible life of the Spirit? Life in the Spirit is juxtaposed with life in the flesh in Galatians 5.20-21. Consider Paul's description of the Spirit-filled life beautifully rendered in the Amplified Bible:

> But the fruit of the Spirit [the result of His presence within us] is love [unselfish concern for others], joy, [inner] peace, patience [not the ability to wait, but how we act while waiting], kindness, goodness, faithfulness

gentleness, self-control. Against such things there is no law. And those who belong to Christ Jesus have crucified the sinful nature together with its passions and appetites. If we [claim to] live by the [Holy] Spirit, we must also walk by the Spirit [with personal integrity, godly character, and moral courage—our conduct empowered by the Holy Spirit].

(Galatians 5.22-25, AMP)

The believer then is empowered to love God and the love of neighbor.

Conclusion

The grace-gathered community encourages the believers' new walk in the life of the Spirit. It is more than becoming a religious community of moral good, although the Spirit produces those virtues. It is life at its best, as God intended. Empowerment to overcome! It is life in the fullness of God. His presence among His people in this world.

The Spirit's power lives in the ministry of His church in the world. His spirit empowers and anoints the preaching of His Word, Christ-exalting anthems of praise, and effective gospel ministry in the world. It is expressed in a handshake, a word of encouragement, and or around the Lord's table, or washing the saint's feet. The Spirit is at work in the body of Christ. It is the breath of God in the life of a congregation. What a joy!

A spirit-filled life is attractive in a world that is broken and ruined. Love and joy are qualities that all people desire. You are heaven's joy on earth in a world of earthly woes. God meets us with nothing less than Himself in them. Where He is present, there is love, joy, and peace!

God chooses to not only walk with us. He desires to meet with His gathered body–the grace-gathering. He pitches His tent among us. That's a good reason to be present when the church gathers. Jesus favors His church with His mighty presence.

The Sacred Alignment in Marriage

Chapter Thirteen

Ephesians 5.17-33

Marriage has fallen on hard times in every way today. Prospective couples sometimes view marriage as too cumbersome and restrictive. They assume that cohabitation is a better option especially if the relationship does not work out. But nothing could be farther from the truth. Research indicates that it undermines both the strength and stability of marriage and family and weakens culture.

Married couples struggle to maintain faithfulness and fidelity in their commitment and navigate the relational ebbs and flows of the terrain. The casualties of divorce are everywhere, and even in the grace-gathered community. Relationally wounded couples need a grace-gathered community. It is their potential for hope and healing.

This once-solid social structure is changing and being re-defined in secular terms today. The fact is that Satan hates what marriage represents. The world separates it from its biblical constructs and exploits it as a means of self-expression and individual freedom. Does the Bible have anything to say about marriage and how it is to work? It sure does.

The Divine Design

God is the designer of marriage, as the traditional ceremony says, "in the ancient bowers of Eden." It created that Adam would not be alone. God's grace extended in the community of the husband and wife, reflecting their communion with God, who also dwells in the unified community called the Godhead.

The first sacred established institution was not the church but marriage and family. Adam (being male) and Eve (being female) were biologically designed by natural order "to be fruitful and multi- ply." They were a couple in covenant with God and one another.

Christian marriage is distinctly called "holy" matrimony! It is a covenant of exclusive love between a male-husband and female-wife characterized by sacrifice and self-giving. God desires that couples live in harmonious union with Him and one another. God intended that marriage on earth reflect the harmony of heaven. Marriage became a "war zone" of landmines, conflicts, and battles after their fall into sin.

That is why Paul describes the importance of the Holy Spirit's filling believers, as we explored in the previous lesson. The greatest happiness in marriage involves the couple's holy consecration unto God. Harmony in the home is possible when the life of God lives out in the home life.

A Spirit-Filled Marriage

What are the characteristics of a spirit-filled marriage? Paul characterizes the spirit-filled life as being brought under the controlling influence of the Holy Spirit. Recognizing Christ's Lordship and yielding ourselves to the Holy Spirit means a Christian marriage can display God's love. This daily surrender depends upon God's work in the day-to-day stuff of life.

> And do not be drunk with wine, which leads to riotous living; but be filled with the Spirit; Speaking to yourselves in psalms and hymns and spiritual songs, singing and making melody in your heart to the Lord; Giving thanks always for all things unto God and the Father in the name of our Lord Jesus Christ; Submitting yourselves one to another in the fear of God.
> (Ephesians 5.18-21 KJBT)

Aligned Together

Paul affirms what scholars now designate as the "household code."[1] The biblical term of submission *hupotasso* is seen negatively in modern culture. For the staunch individualist, it sounds like blind, mindless obedience, being without a voice, or cowering to the harsh male-dominated cultural view of marriage that characterized Roman life.

Paul admonished that men should not treat harshly their wives and embitter them to anger (cf. Colossians 3.19). In the Roman culture, women had little or no input into the legal family matters. Women had very few rights unless they were in the equestrian ruling class, although it was changing at this time.[2] Regardless, Paul's view of mutual submission is counter-cultural to the Roman perspective on women in marriage.

The idea of biblical submission is that both the husband and wife are equal but bear different responsible roles. Mutual submission is an essential aspect of being conformed to the image of Christ. In prayer, a couple prioritizes seeking God's will over things they would otherwise find conflicts about. They seek the mind of the Holy Spirit and come to conclusions together.

The Christ-centered couple submits to God first and to one another in love. There is music in the home because there is a melody in your heart prompted by the Holy Spirit in your communication. An attitude of gratitude for one another as God's gracious gift characterizes a healthy marriage. Marriage is the perfect arena to test the dynamic function of the fruit of the spirit.

A little bit of heaven on earth is possible for struggling marriages. Life's ebbs and flows beat against the vessel of marriage. God's life graciously works in marriage through the Spirit. Such a marriage reflects God's intention for the function of His church.

---

[1] Clinton, Arnold, Zondervan's Exegetical Commentary on Ephesians, Grand Rapids, 2010, 628.
[2] Ibid., p. 645.

Designed Roles

The idea of submission is best understood as a military term, being as an alignment under the authority of another. It is used in terms of roles and responsibilities and not in means of importance or value. Jesus was equal with the Father in essence. He is God the Son. Yet, his role was subordinate, aligned, and in submission to the Father's will.

Wife's Role

Paul's attention now turns to the wife's role.

> Wives, submit yourselves unto your own husbands, as unto the Lord. For the husband is the head of the wife, even as Christ is the head of the church: and he is the savior of the body. Therefore, as the church is subject unto Christ, so let the wives be to their own husbands in everything. (Ephesians 5. 22-24, KJBT)

In the home, submission recognizes the God-appointed role and the husband's massive responsibility in godly leadership. Greek scholars here point out that the term submission is in the middle voice, implying this is a voluntary choice of the woman.[3] In other words, the wife chooses to align herself under God's design. Wives are not in servitude to husbands or without a voice in the decision-making. She recognizes and honors the God-given role of the husband.[4]

The wife is to be treated respectfully as an equal in the home. She is uniquely equipped to fulfill a role that husbands have little or no ability to perform. She was created uniquely for her God-given role. Both in the teachings of Jesus and Paul, women were elevated and valued. It was a much higher place than the cultural norm. They both recognized and appreciated the nature and uniqueness of feminine roles.

Christ is the head of the church, and the husband is likewise the family's spiritual leader. The alignment under the husband is for protective guidance, care, safety, and well-being of the wife. The wife should resist becoming domineering and controlling. Manipulation and

---

[3] Ibid., p. 645.
[4] Ibid., p. 645.

complaint undermine marital satisfaction. She is to respect and admire her husband for his role in the family.

A small but influential minority of equestrian upper-class women were abandoning their maternal instincts and embracing more sexually promiscuous pursuits.[5] Paul's teaching counters this cultural influence and encourages the wife's maternal instinct congruent with natural law. She respects the husband's role and responsibility and lovingly encourages him toward godly leadership.

Husbands' Role

Paul now turns his attention to the husband's role. He addresses the gravity of the husband's responsibility as the spiritual leader in the family. Paul lists both the quality and influence of godly leadership. His admonishment to the average husband in Ephesus would have been counterculture to the strong-handed male domination that characterized the Roman culture.

> Husbands, love your wives, even as Christ also loved the church, and gave himself for it; That he might sanctify and cleanse it with the washing of water by the word, That he might present it to himself a glorious church, not having spot, or wrinkle, or any such thing; but that it should be holy and without blemish. Men should love their wives as their own bodies. He who loves his wife loves himself. For no man ever yet hated his own flesh; but nourishes and cherishes it, even as the Lord the church: (Ephesians 5. 25-29, KJBT)

The godly husband is a responsible servant-leader in the home. We get insight into how the husband faithfully leads the family, just as Christ lovingly leads the church. Paul lays out four distinct leadership qualities.

Spiritual Leadership

How did Jesus spiritually lead His disciples? Jesus was on a mission of seeking and saving the lost. His driving motivation was doing the will

---

[5] Ibid., p. 637-638.

of His heavenly Father. Jesus was very passionate about the will of the Father. He often slipped away in secret prayer, peaking His disciples' interest in His devotional habits and what He talked to His Father about. He agonized in a garden concerning a bitter cup and submitting to the Father's will. His disciples understood the spiritual passion of Jesus was doing His Father's will.

The spiritual husband is to walk in humble obedience. The spiritual leader is passionate about the will of God. He seeks God's purpose, direction, and will in all things. Prayer is a priority for the spirit-led husband as he lives the value of relationships, especially his relationship with His wife. For him, loving servant leadership begins in the home. God's will and purpose are vibrant in the microcosm of such a home.

Passionate serving leadership leads the wife and family in a passion for Christ. He is neither arrogant nor pompous; instead, as a gentleman, he considers his leadership a sacred trust given by the Lord. He does not demand authority but exemplifies submissive dependence upon the Lord. He does not lead out of compulsion, but his life, attitude, and love reflect Christ in the home. Such leadership compels the wife and children to love and follow Christ. His enjoyment is the Lord lived for all to see.

Sacrificial

As Christ loves the church, the husband is to love his wife. He models sacrificial leadership. How did Jesus love the church? Jesus' love was sacrificial and forgiving. It was an abundant, merciful outpouring of His loving favor upon and within His people. Jesus builds and strengthens the church. His love for the church is greater than the evils of hell. Jesus' love is over-the-top grace, reaching out to the rejected, healing the broken, and restoring the alienated. His love covers sins and goes beyond the second mile. People are amazed and feel deeply valued.

Consider how "loving as Christ loves the church" seems utterly impossible. It is certainly not within the natural inclination of the flesh. Pride and ego sacrificed! A desire for dominating control submitted to Christ as Lord. The husband considers his wife's needs over his own. God desires a heart perfectly submissive to the Lord, where He can love her in such a way.

There is no perfect husband, only a perfect Lord whose love is perfecting the husband. Personal confession of sin, receiving and granting forgiveness, and turning away from what destroys our lives and marriages characterize sacrificial leadership. Love and mercy are God's favor fleshed out in relationships.

Sanctifying

How was Jesus a sanctifying leadership displayed before His disciples? Sanctification means consecration or being set apart as holy and wholly unto the Lord. Jesus sent His disciples into the world, but they were to be unspotted from the world through His word. Jesus' great prayer for His disciples in John 17 reveals His heart for His disciples to be cleansed and spotless, just as His desire for believers to share in His glory.

> I do not pray that You should take them out of the world, but that You should keep them from the evil one. They are not of the world, just as I am not of the world. Sanctify them by Your truth. Your word is truth. As You sent Me into the world, I also have sent them into the world. And for their sakes I sanctify Myself, that they also may be sanctified by the truth.
> (John 17.15-19, NKJV)

Jesus sanctified Himself. In other words, He lived a life of purity in pursuit of the truth of Scripture before his disciples. He prayed for their protection from the Evil One and set them apart in their mind, emotions, will, lifestyle, and pursuits by the truth of God's Word. How does a man walk in purity before the Lord? By taking heed to God's Word. A steady spiritual diet in God's word is both purifying and cleansing.

The sanctifying leadership of the marriage and home is set apart unto God and regards the relationship as a sacred union. It says that there is something special about the relationship. The husband has the great honor of communicating in such a way that she understands her value to him. Words of affirmation and actions that express the depth of love and genuine care. It does not treat the union as mundane and ordinary, but it is revered, sacred, and celebrated.

What do you consecrate then for your marriage? Set apart conversations to discuss God's work within your life and your marriage. You set aside time for talking with each other. Share stories, memories, goals, dreams, desires, and what makes up life. You set aside time to cultivate dreams and work together. Make some dreams come true through planning. Set aside some of your finances for building up your marriage through date nights and getaways.

Like Jesus has consecrated the church unto purity and holiness, you can joyfully consecrate your marriage to Christ. When Christ is the unseen guest and purifying influence of the family, He is most glorified. Every home needs an open Bible and hearts eager to hear, read, and discuss its precepts. It has a purifying influence. Jesus will one day present a Bride before his Father without spot or blemish from this world. Jesus is our sanctifying truth.

Servant Leadership

How did Jesus serve his disciples and others? He taught that the greatest in the kingdom is the servant. (cf. Mark 10.45) The servant did not demand personal rights but one of serving in menial tasks. So, Jesus, and the Passover meal, kneels and washes his disciples' feet. Power, prestige, and prominence are the world's standard modes of operation. God's kingdom operates through humble service. Humble service expects nothing in return or keeps accounts. It freely gives, with no strings attached. The purest act of serving is a beautiful offering of worship before God.

The husband seeks meaningful ways of serving his wife. He nourishes his wife and strengthens her emotionally, spiritually, and physically. A godly husband builds her up in every way so that she can be and become everything God created for her. Nourish her God-given and God-honoring talents and dreams and support her saying "yes" to God's purpose and will for her life. Servant leadership asks, "How can I practically serve you where you feel your immense value?"

Serving leadership cherishes her immeasurable value. Cherish is a tenderness that keeps her warm. It does not talk or treat harshly but rather tenderly. A wife finds security (her great need) in an attentive husband who leads through humility and love. Love creates an environment of acceptance that creates a peaceful home environment. As beautiful flowers grow in soil that is nurtured and given attention, so does a happy home. Marriage can be either a battlefield where there is a continual struggle for control or a sweet surrender to the Lord and one another.

Aligned as One With Christ

The church is under Christ in her submission and unified under Christ's headship of the body. It is the mystery of the church. Paul compares Christian marriage with the mystery of the Church. As the husband and wife are one flesh, the church body is in a covenant oneness with God.

> For we are members of his body, of his flesh, and of his bones. For this cause shall a man leave his father and mother, and shall be joined unto his wife, and the two shall be one flesh. This is a great mystery: but I speak concerning Christ and the church. Nevertheless let every one of you in particular love his wife even as himself; and the wife see that she respects her husband.
> (Ephesians 5. 30-33, KJBT)

We are His" flesh and bones" in this world–inhabited by His Spirit. The church is one. It is one under Christ as the church's head, being one in purpose in multiple spiritual gifts. Bringing glory to the heavenly Father, the church is aligned with Christ, fulfilling Jesus's prayer of making believers one. (cf. John 17)

Husbands and wives leave their mother and father and become one in body, soul, and spirit. The church is called out from the world to be the body of Christ in this world. The church is the bride of Christ, awaiting the marriage supper of the lamb.

Conclusion

The church is the one institution that stands in support of strong marriages and families. Called to the biblical precepts, teaching Scripture instructs and strengthens the families. The strength of the family is vital for church health and the unseen moral fabric of a civil community. Our communities need strong families.

The church stands as a guardian of the sanctity of biblical marriage. Preserving traditional marriage is essential for a stable society, especially considering the prevailing confusion and misdirection of the culture. The grace-gathering has a unique opportunity to nurture and protect the family and encourage the crucial role of fathers and mothers in raising an upcoming generation.

Survival Basics for the Family

Chapter Fourteen

Ephesians 6.1-4

There has never been a more critical time for the family than today. With every fractured and broken family, the social cohesion of society weakens. Teachers, administrators, and social workers in numerous agencies try to pick up the pieces of fragmented lives and bring order to the chaos. These issues are complex and perplexing. Children seek and long to belong, and they will meet their needs from a positive or negative source. Precious children act up and act out often because of deep emotional, social, personal, or spiritual needs.

A healthy family unit provides an emotional sense of belonging and security. A strong family unit begins with building a healthy marriage, and a Christ-aligned marriage of predictability establishes a sense of security. The best thing you can give your children is a strong marriage. You are modeling marriage for the upcoming generation and laying a foundation for them to follow.

Your family feels the pressures of juggling work schedules, increasing demands on your time, and growing expectations of the household, health, and finances. You feel it as stress! What are some scriptural guidelines that help you protect the most sacred trust– your family?

If you are not intentionally engaged in "thought-out parenting," you find yourself outsourcing your presence in the family to phones, iPads, or video games. Demands are ever increasing upon you and your family. How do you relieve some stress and put some margin into your family schedule? Slowing the maddening pace and the suffocating influences stressing the family feels like you are on a runaway train. It's just difficult to stop or slow down. The fast life is affecting your children, and some research points out that children benefit from the opportunities presented by slowing down. Amazingly, boredom just might be the spark of imagination and develop analytical skills. Bless your children with free playtime. They will find greater enjoyment in creative play than "screen time."

The Roman Family

Christian household code not only elevated the role of women in Roman culture but also the value of children. In the typical Roman family, the father maintained total control over his wife, children, slaves, and property. He had legal authority over all family affairs and the final word over his children as long as he was alive. A Roman father could sell their children into slavery. Even small unwanted children were left abandoned in the marketplace if the father wished.

With the weakened state of marriage in the empire, the enterprise of temple prostitution was the accepted practice. With sexual immorality prevalent, especially among men, children would have been unwelcomed and unwanted. The custom included a child presented at the father's feet. If the father walked away, then the child was left in the Roman forum at night. These children were deprived of the security of a loving family, sold into slavery and among the brothels.[1]

Sadly, women and children always suffer the most in a culture driven by sensual pleasure. As depraved practices deepened, the social structures weakened. As the family unit weakens in America, a massive rise of neglected and abused children suffer in wait for a stable family life, and social breakdown closely follows. Only a return to the biblical foundation of marriage will strengthen our country. This is the hope for failing social institutions that cannot bear the weight of what's broken in the family.

Survival Basics

Although no two families are the same, the ancient wisdom of Scripture provides the foundation for a stable family life. Many of the stressors upon the family today would be relieved if husbands and wives would align the priority and value of the family unit with sacred principles. Let

---

[1] William Barclay's, The Daily Bible Study, The Letters to Galatians & Ephesians, Westminster Press, 1958, 210-211.

us explore briefly the concepts of alignment and esteem and specific principles for strengthening the family. Paul draws upon the wisdom from Exodus 20.12.

Let us explore these time-proven principles in these four power-packed verses.

> Children, obey your parents in the Lord: for this is right. Honor your father and mother; (which is the first commandment with promise). That it may be well with you and that you may live long on the earth. And fathers do not provoke your children to wrath: but bring them up in the nurture and admonition of the Lord.
> (Ephesians 6.1-4, KJBT)

Aligns in God's Design

Paul calls children to obey their parents. As the husband and wife model mutual submission to Christ and align their lives in their God-given roles, the children align themselves under the protective hedge of the family. A child needs a secure environment to grow up and healthily mature physically, mentally, emotionally, and spiritually.

We desire our children to grow into mature, responsible adults who love God and others as Christ. It is a worthy goal of a Christian home. Healthy families nurture such growth. It could rightly be called the Grace Gathering at home. The term obedience here *hupakos*– means "to hearken to a command." It carries the weight of listening and applying godly instruction to every aspect of life.

The children of Israel were to observe the commandments in the law of Moses. A life of obedience looks like loving God. Walking, clinging to God, and serving him characterize a love for God. (cf. Joshua 22.5) Characteristics of the last days include a pervasive "disobedience to parents." This last-day scenario describes a time lacking the natural affection of love. The "end times" are characterized by love waxing cold!

Most parents wish that their children just conform to the behavioral demands. Behavior within the socially acceptable rules and guidelines helps us "save face" among our peers. Strict compliance with family rules sometimes produces just the opposite in children. Little hearts can seethe in resentment, planting a seed of rebellion and a bitter fruit later. In actuality, we want something more from our children. We desire obedience motivated by love and respect. Obedience is a better motivation than compliance because it draws from a loving relationship. That is why Jesus said, If you love me, keep my words.

Esteem Family & Home Life

The family is sacred. God created a family for the social structure of raising children. Although Christian parents are rightly concerned about the outside influences that potentially shape their children's character, the family unit is more influential in the long run than the changing fads of culture. As technology and travel expands, adults and children can carelessly drift to an island of isolation.

It is much easier to escape in the world of your phone, television, or computer and lay aside the much-needed relational work. Healthy relationships take time and hard work, requiring difficult conversations, understanding "hurt feelings," deeper commitments, and forgiveness. The fuel of our hurry-up life has us grabbing fast food on the way to the next event. We are losing something more.

The lack of deep and meaningful conversations with our children suffers. The internal questions of eternity arise from our children when they have time to think. Meaningful God-centered conversations flow out of relational investments in our children. The family team needs the esteem!

God intends the home to be a safe place and sanctuary for handling the issues of life. Parents have home-field advantage in the game of life. Make the home a safe landing spot, even after the children leave the nest. How does that happen? Let's look.

Integrate by Modeling Obedience

Paul admonished, Children, obey your parents in the Lord: for this is right. (Ephesians 6.1)

Paul relays the first principle of modeling obedience. It does not happen by barking out commands at the children but by modeling the value of family before their eyes. It is more caught than taught. The power of persuasion lies in what you love and how you live. Esteem family togetherness and home life rather than being on the constant go, the children get the message clearly and feel it as security. Christian parents integrate this in two interconnected ways.

A Growing Spiritual Life

Modeling a growing, vibrant spiritual walk in the Lord establishes a deeper spiritual dynamic in the family. Children should obey their parents *in the Lord,* according to verse one. I have often heard that Christ is the unseen guest of the Christian home. The awareness of His presence and life set the tone for the family. His purposes integrated into the life and activity, the passions and dreams, and the very heart of the family.

The grace-gathered community supports grace-filled parenting and homes. The church supports parents, not by adding more activity to an already "way too-busy" lifestyle but by integrating personal devotion and spiritual growth in daily life and activities. As the family grows together in Christ, spiritual life becomes the core of family life. Growing up in Christlikeness always makes for a better family. When planning your family schedule, model the importance of community through the church. It not only lasts a lifetime, but relationships go right into eternity.

A Deepening Moral Consciousness

The implications of the phrase "it is right" are monumental. It is an established morality based upon something absolute. What is absolute conveys what is right or the standard. It is based upon more than a subjective feeling but reflects a moral reality. It aligns with Scripture and the function of a moral universe.

Paul establishes the truth that informs the conscience and helps children mature spiritually, socially, and naturally. Children learn early on the importance of sharing toys and getting along. It becomes an instilled value that informs their conscience.

You help teach and shape that as a parent. Children learn that every human being reflects the image of God and is worthy of value and respect. God has entrusted us with a great responsibility to be a part of the human family. Such an awareness will serve them at every stage of life and in every relationship.

Mending relationships is important through saying, "I'm sorry." They learn that empathy and understanding are valuable and that life does not revolve around themselves and what they always want. Hearing, listening, and learning other's needs are essential in interpersonal dynamics. They grow in the capacity to both receive and extend forgiveness.

A moral consciousness helps them discern between right and wrong, sort out and manage priorities, and regulate the influences of their peer group. Later in life, they will learn to evaluate and discern complex moral and ethical issues.

An informed conscience shaped through the time-proven principles of Scripture brings the eternal into perspective. A conscience informed by God's Word stabilizes the soul against momentary pressures they face or guards their heart desires. It will serve them well into adulthood.

Honor What Lasts Forever

Honor your father and mother; (which is the first commandment with promise). That it may be well with you and that you may live long on the earth. (Ephesians 6.3)

Family honor was so important in the collective Mediterranean culture. Bringing shame to the family name was avoided at all costs. In Roman society, the oldest living father held the legal authority over the whole family. He made the final decision affecting the family. The Father set the tone of the family.

If the Father was harsh and overbearing, pressure for compliance was felt on the sons. The family name was at stake. The family was always mindful of preserving family honor through acceptable behavior to the family code. As you can imagine, it was often strict compliance without satisfying loving relationships within the family. That would vary from family to family.

Relationships are Forever

Western culture has a different approach. Family at least has been valued highly because of its Judeo-Christian foundations, but culture is gravitating toward finding personal happiness through individual expression now.

Individual expression sometimes conflicts with the expected norms and behaviors the parents uphold. At times, a child's actions or outbursts cause deep parental concern. Parents worry if their child will turn out "ok." Behavior is usually an indicator of deeper spiritual, emotional, or relational needs that require attention. Communication helps mend relational fences and build bridges to understanding. The wise parent looks deeper than behavior and aims toward the heart of the relationship. A Christian parent desires that their child grow in love and maturity through an obedient heart to Christ.

Honor *timeo* is a biblical teaching about values. The Ten Commandments are sacred. What is sacred is valuable. Human relationships are eternal and have eternal value. People want to know that they are cared for and are valued. The most basic human relationships are between father, mother, brother, and sister. We should esteem relationships from one generation to the next. Relationships are forever.

Positions, power, wealth, prestige, homes, lands, and careers change and fade away. Death sobers us up and reminds us that these things don't last forever. We are left only with relationships–with God and one another. God blesses the family where loving one another is practiced. Now, this is a legacy to pass down generationally. Make it a family tradition, and leave your children's children a blessing!

Establish Loving Limits

The family feels pressure from every front today. From the world system to the cultural influences, the world's message and preferences are shaping the minds and hearts of our children. It happens often and daily through screen time. Our chaotic schedules make life feel like it is unraveling. It just might help fuel the anxiety within the children.

The Ten Commandments are sacred and provide the basic moral guidelines for prioritizing and ordering our spiritual and social life. It begins with a spiritual order to have no other gods before Yahweh. The fifth commandment deals with our social life. It begins with honoring God and establishing loving limits in protecting the sacredness of those relationships. These commandments help direct the conscience to prioritize the value of relationships. Teach and schedule "loving limits." How do you establish these? Discern what is a season of life and prioritize what lasts forever.

I'm afraid we use the term family too loosely today. While in high school, I thought that a sense of closeness and belonging with schoolmates would be forever. Graduation brought massive changes to those relationships. After we tossed our caps at graduation, we scattered in many directions. It was a season of life. You realize this at your 20-year reunion, where you struggle to remember names and how much life has changed.

Livelihood consumes much of our time and attention. Work demands the investment of a lot of time to tasks with people. The closeness of proximity creates a "family-like" feeling. But even if our job and vocation involve 30 to 40 years, work associates are not family proper. Retirement brings a change in those relationships.

Sports consume a lot of family time today. Massive amounts of money today are invested in learning a game and all the trappings that surround the momentary game. It is big business with some sports. But, at the end of the sports season, these relationships are usually seasonal.

I cannot tell you how to prioritize your time and how you spend it, but the biblical foundation nurtures the eternal nature and value of relationships in the family unit. The church and family are the only institutions on earth that are not seasonal or transient.

It's easy to put the church gathering on the back burner. Attendance gets scheduled out. We say that when this season in my life passes, I will establish and grow the spiritual roots that nurture a healthy morality. The message is clear to our children. The spiritual influences are optional. It is not hard to see how a nominal and optional faith in one generation leads to a generation that "deconstructs" their faith altogether and rejects Christian morality. It is a natural regression!

Do Not Exasperate Morale

Fathers have the unique opportunity to keep the fires stokes for a child's internal motivation for what is good and right. *And fathers do not provoke your children to wrath: but bring them up in the nurture and admonition of the Lord.* (Ephesians 6.4)

Wise teachers understand and know the power of words. The right words can empower motivation within the human spirit or crush any internal drive. Relationships based solely upon behavior make the quality of love feel dependent on behavior and conditional.

Criticism and rejection become etched into our children's minds like a broken record, and they view themselves as failures and their future dreadful. Even the encouraging words of parents and others pale to the blare of negative self-talk. Regardless, get them into the steady flow of Scripture to guide them. They will certainly need it.

The Fire in the Eyes

Paul admonishes the father, do not provoke the children. Don't provoke them through harsh and excessive demands that were the norm of the Roman father. Biblical fatherhood is like the family shepherd caring for and guiding the family. The father can help the family (sheep) follow his relational steps. Don't be the cause of their discouragement.

Develop relational consistency through deep spiritual roots that build them up. Words are most impactful when they are from a strong relationship and time spent together. Fan the flame of the child's natural talents and abilities. Aid them in discovering the truth of themselves as God views them. What a responsibility for Christian parents today!

Fan the Flame

Fan the flame of nurturing spiritual maturity. Parents are to "bring the children up." It is consistent and intentional parenting. Do not cripple your children, either emotionally or spiritually, but bring them up by lifting them in the truth. Help them understand the nature of God!

They will understand themselves more clearly, including their deep spiritual need and what arises within them that is prone to sin. Give them a vision of how they can flourish in relationships and life. Fan the flame of their mental and natural skills through hands-on learning opportunities. Bring your children up by bringing them alongside you.

Nurturing and training fan the flame. Impact their lives through practical and encouraging instruction. Show them how to live for God, the importance of prayer and the altar, the Bible and study, and serving God in ministry through the grace-gathered body of the church. Teach them how to deal with the pressures of time and conflicts through forgiveness.

Creativity flourishes in a nurturing home environment. A child learns to play a musical instrument. She develops writing skills. He works in the hands-on application of creating things. Sporting events are a microcosm of life. These competitions teach children emotional control, dealing with disappointment, success, teamwork, and how to master themselves –mind, soul, body, spirit, and emotion.

Being intentional in passing down the faith to the next generation requires moral and spiritual instruction–admonition. It is wise counsel and instruction either through correcting reproof or encouragement. Admonishment leads people to Christ as the firm footing for a forward-moving life.

Relationally involved parenting is the groundwork for understanding the needs of our children. Nothing fans the spiritual flames more than the word of God, which brings correction through the conviction of sin through the Holy Spirit's comforting encouragement in dealing with difficulties.

Conclusion

The grace-gathered community seeks to strengthen the family unit. It supports the divine design of marriage, home, and family. No earthly institution matches the importance of marriage, family, and the church. At their core are relationships!

The study of the Scripture helps parents navigate the family through the landmines of an ever-increasing secular culture. The grace-gathered church is there to support you. Our children are too important for us to recoil into passivity or a laissez-faire attitude. We have the all-too-important role of raising a generation that learns the spiritual foundation of life in Christ. In that regard, we should lovingly and earnestly pray for one another and strengthen the family within the church and broken families in the culture. God bless the family!

Love is patient and kind;
love does not envy or boast;
It is not arrogant or rude.
It does not insist on its own way;
it is not irritable or resentful;
it does not rejoice at wrongdoing,
but rejoices with the truth.
Love bears all things,
believes all things,
hopes all things,
endures all things.
Love never fails!

~1 Corinthians 13. 4-7 (ESV)

*Not with eyeservice, as men-pleasers,
but as bondservants of Christ,
doing the will of God
from the heart, with goodwill
doing service, as to the Lord,
and not to men, knowing
that whatever good anyone does,
he will receive the same
from the Lord,
whether he is a slave or free.*

Colossians 3.7-8, (KJBT)

Working Principles for the Workplace

Chapter Fifteen

Ephesians 6.5-9

The power of God's gracious kindness is life-changing. Spiritual change happens for those receiving this freeing grace. It secures our identity in Christ and frees us to serve God and seek His will with pure motivation. It lives out in a radical love for others. A believer converts from a self-centered life to living under Christ's Lordship. He is Lord over all our life: in what we think, how we feel, and what we do, whether in our home, church, or workplace.

Is the supremacy of Christ the alignment and motivation of our work? Work is one way of serving the Creator. Remember that God gave Adam and Eve in the garden the responsibility of naming the animal kingdom and cultivating the garden paradise. Part of the curse was the garden would produce thorns, and they would toil among the thistles.

There is a direct correlation between work and providing for our family. Work strikes the nerve of life's purpose and meaning intuitively within us. We are hardwired for more than making money because money does not bring ultimate fulfillment. Money may provide happier moments, more opportunities, and pleasant experiences, but money cannot create satisfaction in the human spirit. Meaning is a much deeper inclination of the soul search.

> Bondservants, be obedient to those who are your masters according to the flesh, with fear and trembling, in sincerity of heart, as to Christ; not with eyeservice, as men-pleasers, but as bondservants of Christ, doing the will of God from the heart, with goodwill doing service, as to the Lord, and not to men, knowing that whatever good anyone does, he will receive the same from the Lord, whether *he is* a slave or free. And you, masters, do

the same things to them, giving up threatening, knowing that your own Master also is in heaven, and there is no partiality with Him. (Ephesians 6. 5-9, KJBT)

First-Century Slavery[1]

Paul addressed a culture where slavery was an accepted economic and social construct. First-century slavery in the Roman Empire was unlike our understanding of slavery with the ethnic dimension in our national history. The buying and selling of human beings as personal property derives from the depth of human depravity. It is unjustifiable and morally wrong. Paul did not address slavery as a system. He went for the heart of people. With spiritual change, moral convictions align with God, and social systems structure toward justice. In nations where the gospel advances, the practice of slavery eventually crumbles. Why? Injustice and greed is the heart issue that must first bow to Christ's Lordship. There are no class divisions at the cross, just equal sinners needing grace.

Both slave and master created in the image of God are created equal and bow at the same altar, and Christ is the Lord over all. Paul did not focus on Christianizing a pagan Roman culture or reforming a broken system. He focused on the Kingdom of God among the kingdoms of this world. The gospel makes us new. This gospel calls out the broken ones to the blessing of new life and a different way of living.

The Roman Empire did not have a middle class as we understand it. The economic structure included a small percentage of the ruling equestrian class, with one-third of the population being slaves. The slave population consisted of conquered people groups or those financially destitute.

Some slaves were well-educated. Some worked in medicine, teaching professions, and various skilled labors. But the slaves had given up their rights. They were marked and owned by their masters. As you can imagine, masters could be kind and benevolent, while some were harsh and abusive. Slaves could be bought out of their slavery and become freemen.

---

[1] See Arnold, P. 715-720

Interestingly, Paul refers to himself as a bondservant *doulos* of Christ. He had given up rights to himself to the life of Christ, the most kindly gracious Master. The greatest in God's kingdom is the servant-*doulos*. That describes leadership in God's economy. The greatest among you is your servant.

Who Do You Work For?

How often have you been asked where you are employed? There is an assumption in the question. We have an employer who may or may not provide a sustainable income. Regardless, you voluntarily align with a company, agency, business, or organization providing an income. But the real question remains, "Who are you working for?"

Some might answer that they work for the family business or in a career or vocation. Some might say they work for a paycheck, which is the lowest level of satisfaction in the work-related question. Others work to provide for themselves, build careers, or grow nest eggs.

We have a created purpose, and work helps us find meaning. Many struggle to re-orient life to purpose and meaning when their work status changes. We all work and have an underlying motivation for our work. How we answer that question often reveals the depth of what drives and motivates us in our purpose. So, who are you working for?

Even in our church or volunteer work, we must answer this question. Leadership requires answering the questions of motivation of why we do what we do and for whom. So perhaps a better question is," Who am I working for?"

Rightly answering these questions is crucial. The Scripture describes the highest aspiration for our work and the motivation to work well. We intuitively know that the value of work involves more than a paycheck, even though a good one sure eases some burdens in life.

Deeper Heart Motivation

Within the Ephesian church, there were both slaves and masters. In the new community of grace, everyone is equal and feels valued, even though their income and position may have placed them in unequal economic situations. Money and status do not make anyone valuable. Personal value is intrinsic to being human.

At the heart of motivation for work is knowing who you are working for! Work environments can be a source of great satisfaction or hand-wringing stress. But at the heart of work, who are you serving? Work is an opportunity to show that you are working for or serving Christ. Your job is the opportunity to show how Jesus would do your work.

So, bondservants were called to respect the structured authority, as difficult as that might be. We serve the Lord with fear and trembling. Just like you are accountable for your job responsibility to your supervisor, you bear an even greater and ultimate responsibility to the Lord.

Doing your work as unto the Lord is the purest motivation for work! This attitude positions you to do your best work. We are ultimately accountable to the Lord, giving an account to Him. Our jobs and ministries all belong to Him. Living in that reality makes for a satisfying work experience.

Paul reminds the Corinthian believers that there is a coming judgment of the believer's works. The church will gather in heaven, and the *bema* judgment rewards follow. The believer's work and motivation behind his work will be "tested by fire. The purity of the believer's works is exposed. Our work will receive its proper reward.

> Now if anyone builds on this foundation with gold, silver, precious stones, wood, hay, straw, each one's work will become clear; for the Day will declare it, because it will be revealed by fire; and the fire will test each one's work, of what sort it is. If anyone's work which he has built on it endures, he will receive a reward. If anyone's work is burned, he will suffer loss; but he himself will be saved, yet so as through fire.
> (1 Corinthians 3.12, NKJV)

All work is an opportunity to serve the Lord, and God alone knows our motivation. So, he reminds believers that pure service is humbly given in "fear and trembling" and with the utmost singleness of heart. It is service honestly rendered without pretense, as to the Lord. Perhaps a better question "How is your work of the Lord going?" Why? Christ is really on trial in your workplace!

Higher Sights of Focus

Sometimes, I focus on people and things more than God. I recognize my tendency. There is an old cliche that someone is so heavenly-minded that they are of no earthly good. I don't think that is the case today in a culture that seeks meaning and relevance immediately. If anything, we are too earthly-minded and self-focused.

It is indeed tragic, especially for the church, that endeavors to lift our eyes and sights in respect to the Lord on Sunday. Most of us have spent our week looking ahead, behind us, or down. What if we set our sights higher? What if we position our heart and focus more heavenly? What if we rendered our work as a gift to Christ? I believe we would not only be better in our serving, but we would have more satisfaction in working for Jesus.

> Not with eyeservice, as men-pleasers, but as bondservants of Christ, doing the will of God from the heart, with goodwill doing service, as to the Lord, and not to men, knowing that whatever good anyone does, he will receive the same from the Lord, whether *he is* a slave or free. (Colossians 3.7-8, NKJV)

Believers recognize that the master above is watchful of their service. Man-centered work is motivated by what is seen and evaluated only by man. Such motivation seeks to satisfy the minimal work requirement and man's approval. It is a poor motivator.

Will you work for the Lord without notice or the appreciation of people? Will you work for the Lord without expectation or a payoff in some fashion? Will you work for the Lord as a gift given to him out of love?

Is your service a work of goodwill? Is it grace-given enthusiastic service? Negativity and complaining reveal the deeper motivations of the heart and misplaced expectations in serving. Jesus calls us to lay it all aside. He does not need our "perfect work" but heart-rendered service for His glory alone.

Paul reminds the Ephesian believers that the Lord indeed honors faithful service given to Him. Although that is not the motivation, the

Bible does remind us that Jesus is the reward. He knows how to bring deep satisfaction in our souls through obedience in serving.

What we do can make a difference now and in eternity. Recognizing the impact is more than a task we perform, whether mundane or exhilarating, but in the relationships we build along the way. Relationships matter for all eternity, including those formed through work.

Great Value of Relationships

Finally, Paul gives succinct directions for masters. These were the ones who bore the weight of authority of positions over others. The masters were to give up "the threatening"--as common among master-slave relationships.

Onesimus was a runaway slave, and Paul pleads with Philemon by letter to receive him back. Much of this is relational common sense. Treat all people with respect and dignity. People are more valuable than programs, activities, or the tasks they perform. We should seek the best interests of people. There is no place for the abuse of authority in any fashion.

I have had the privilege of working with and under the authority of some great administrators and business owners. I was privileged to observe top-level leaders lead with integrity and character. They garner deep respect and loyalty. They led by influence and did not use their position or authority to demand what they wanted. They were servant leaders.

These leaders placed a great value upon relationships. Even if job specifics did not work out, they focused on the value of the individual and sought what was best for the person. In other words, they lead others with a depth of genuine care, and influence was their power.

These influential leaders articulate the value of people in the organization. They treated them as equals, regardless of their role in the business and the organization. Such leaders gain so much more in the organization. It is not uncommon for employees to work sacrificially and with deep loyalty. Such caring work environments grow caring teams.

Conclusion

There is eternal value in relationships. Let us work with eternity in view. Don't let work become a hindrance to building relationships. May the purest motivation be serving Christ as work unto Christ.

The passion week of Christ was the completion of His work for our salvation. In Jesus' dying hour, He was building relationships with two thieves. They deserved their punishment. One trusted the sufficiency of Christ on the Cross. He took Jesus at His word that he would be with him in paradise.

We will all die with unfinished tasks. May we find meaning in our work and build relationships along the way! Spiritual bridge-building seems small, but it lays a smooth foundation to share the gospel. It is indeed a great work! Relationships were Jesus' passion, even in His dying hour! May it be the purpose of our living days.

Be Strong in the Lord
and in the
power of His might.
Take up the
whole armor of God,
that you may be
able to withstand
in the evil day.

~The Apostle Paul

Winning the War Within

Chapter Sixteen

Ephesians 6.10-18

If the Apostle Paul was writing to the Christians today, what would he say? It is doubtful that it would be much different than the Ephesian's letter. It might sound something like this:

Dear Grace Gathering

I longed to journey with you in your faith but cannot now. Maybe we'll get together soon. So, I'm writing. I pray God's blessing of peace fills your journey. Here are some pointers on the way.

Remember who you are in Christ. He is your new identity.

You have embarked on a marvelous faith journey by entering a relationship with Jesus Christ. God has created you for this relationship with Christ. You are now in Christ, and Christ is living in you. "In Christ," God calls you chosen, holy, blameless, predestined, and adopted as His child. You're in the family!

In one marvelous transaction on Christ's cross, you were bought and freed from the slave market of sin. It's a new day with a new lease on life. So live like the forgiven person you are. He doesn't remember your past, so He can't hold it over your head. So don't you. Don't let your past trip you up. Its grip has been broken and does not define you anymore.

Remember how blessed you are.

Do you know that He put your name on the bank account? The riches that belong to Jesus also belong to you. I am telling you, he counts you as a part of the family. It's a full-fledged, done deal. Go figure, huh? I know it's over the top, but that's "just the way" He is. He delights in you!

By the way, don't worry about trying to prove yourself. It doesn't work with Him. You don't gain acceptance into the family or get your name written into the will by hard work. I know this sounds strange, but when Jesus paid your way–you're in! Your name is listed right there with the rest of your brothers and sisters.

Yes, Jesus' inheritance belongs to you, and I can't wait for you to see it. You cannot imagine how promising your future looks, and I can hardly describe it. You're one rich person, friend!

Remember you have a traveling companion.

Before I forget, He has sent a traveling companion to accompany you. He is like your "seal of the done deal" before He sees you face to face. You're that valuable to him. I know he spared no expense. The fullness of all He is has come and is coming your way, so look out! I would listen closely to your traveling companion's guidance and depend on His strength. You will need him along the journey.

Don't take for granted the treasure that He has given. You see, He feels like you're His treasure also. When I first realized He felt that way about me, my brain threw circuits. I still wonder why! Somehow, it seems it all goes back to Jesus.

Don't get bogged down by your past life.

It will rob you if you let it. You lack nothing in Christ. You have all His fullness as He is above all, in all, and in you. Remember how he saved you by His matchless grace through faith in Christ. You were once in bondage, bound in the chains of sin and held by the prince and power of the air.

You were speeding down the super-highway to hell, headed toward an impending judgment as God's enemy. You were in a fix you couldn't fix. But no more! That life is behind you now, so leave it in the dust. You're traveling on a more narrow road, but it is a better way in the long term. Don't forget it. Believe it or not, you are his handiwork of grace on display! He's proud of what's taking shape!

I am praying that you are growing in love.

I pray that you find strength in the depth of Christ's love. You have a real power to walk in love for others. Take a deep plunge into the depths of

God's love. It's vast and endless. It is refreshing in a cold world. It is deeply satisfying. Don't forget that it helps you to live it out everywhere to everybody. It's a relationship builder! I am surprised how few people get it or live in it. But, love is one more of your Father's rich provisions.

Find Your Place in the Family

His love will help you to live out your new life around everybody. You know how some people can unnerve and unsettle you. But you will grow richest in love as you find your place among the grace-gathered people. Remember you are discovering along with them your Father's loving provision. You are becoming more like your Father daily. I hear of His gracious kindness in you. You're living this grace-filled life in not-so-easy places, like home, school, work, and everywhere. His grace is working in you. It's a sight to see!

Sing loud and joyfully!

It is a new day where His love and life are reigning. You've got plenty to sing about now. His fullness is "smack dab" in the middle of your heart. You eat from a massive fruit bowl of love, joy, and peace. No wonder you sing loud when you gather to worship. I get the reports! You've got every right to. You continue pouring out your heart. It's affecting your marriage and children. Everybody notices something different about you, even the people you work with.

That's why your Father sent the traveling companion. He wanted you to experience the joy in the journey. Just think, every step you take is joy from above. It's God's little reminder that the best is coming. Just wait and see and journey on.

Discover peaceful valleys of beauty, rest, and be nourished by refreshing streams. Your traveling companion was a shepherd who knows the way. You can breathe deeply and rest. Welcome to the Christian Life. It is more than you could ever imagine.

Don't Get Rattled by the Battle

I must tell you this now. There is joy in this journey and be careful not to fall asleep in the comfort of everything. It's easy to doze off when you need to be awake. Remember, the narrow way has piercing thorns, thistles, and dangers unseen, but don't be disturbed by them. You're not home yet. Oh, you will be, but not now.

Most people don't expect this on the journey. Don't let it rattle you. Lurking in the darkness of the narrow path are taunting giants. The giant is large, foreboding, cursing the reality of anything, good or holy. He roars like a lion, and the earth shakes underneath His crushing stomps. As the ground shakes, so will you in your shoes. Just stand till and be quiet.

He is a fierce bully. He will remind you of your past, jeers of guilt penetrate with a foreboding dread of unforgiveness, stabbing fear will stab your heart, and you will weaken feeling your inadequacy. You may even feel like your traveling companion has run out. He has not. He's close by. I promise you that.

You will be disappointed. It's evitable and a part of the journey. You will ask, "Is this the Christian life"? Surely not. The invisible war within you emotionally wears you out. You are in a battle, but don't let it rattle you. Jesus is your champion. I am praying for you. Victory is certain. The grace-gathered family will one day be together. You'll get around to see me, and I want to meet you face to face. I want you to know that you are always in the mind of your Father. I know it's hard to believe, but it is true. Just wait and see, and you'll understand it better one day. Until then,

Grace & Peace

Paul

Hear Paul's answer to the battles we face.

> Finally, my brethren, be strong in the Lord and in the power of His might. Put on the whole armor of God, that you may be able to stand against the wiles of the devil. For we do not wrestle against flesh and blood, but against principalities, against powers, against the rulers of the darkness of this age, against spiritual *hosts* of wickedness in the heavenly *places.*
> (Ephesians 6.10-12, KJBT)

The Bible is replete with battle imagery. The children of Israel faced a certain death at the Red Sea until God parted the water, and they crossed over on dry ground. David stands against a giant. The whole book of Joshua is a conquest to possess the promised land. Paul describes fighting the good fight. Jude contends for the faith. Paul told Timothy to endure hardships like a good soldier. The picture is that the Christian life is not on "easy street" but more like a battle. Paul describes it as an inward battle struggling with the sin nature in the epistle of Romans. Jesus has won your victory, but it's still a battle.

An Enemy Scheming

It is unlike any physical conflict we face. The battle is a spiritual conquest against the fleshly nature that lifts itself as Master and controller of our life. The wiles of the devil are indeed "wiley." (cf. Ephesians 6.11) These wiles *methodeia* are *schemes* of the Evil One. The enemy is scheming opportunities to hinder the work of the Spirit and for you to operate in the flesh. Believers at least need to be aware of Satan's methodical schemes.

Your real enemy controls the way of the world through the lust of flesh and the pride of life. He schemed against Jesus in the wilderness temptation. Rulers *arche* of the spiritual realm, principalities, rulers, or magistracy. Power *exousia* is the cosmic authority of the age. Spiritual darkness is any ungodliness or immorality lurking in the shadows, plotting for us to miss the mark of God's glory. Evil is the wickedness that flows from the depth of depravity. We find ourselves in a war within.

The names of the Evil One give us insight into the source of our battle.

1. Satan is the *adversary* attacks by ambush. Satan was behind all the horrendous evils Job dealt with.

2. The Devil is the diabolical slanderer, throwing falsehoods against someone.

3. The Deceive works through deceptions and lies, blinding minds to the truth of the knowledge of God.

4. Accuser of the Brethren–Satan accuses you before God and God before you.

Paul describes strongholds in what and how we think, what and how we feel, that affect how we live.

Paul is succinct concerning his spiritual battle.

> For though we walk in the flesh, we are not waging war according to the flesh. For the weapons of our warfare are not of the flesh but have divine power to destroy strongholds. We destroy arguments and every lofty opinion raised against the knowledge of God, and take every thought captive to obey Christ, being ready to punish every disobedience, when your obedience is complete. (2 Corinthians 10.3-6, NKJV)

So, the enemy schemes to build a structure in our life. It is the structure of thoughts, feelings, and actions. The actions over time become the habits that control lives, spiritually defeating us and possibly ruining testimonies. It's the stuff that makes us miserable in the long run.

An Empowering Strength

Blockbuster movies gross millions of dollars at the box office. A good novel and movie theme begins with a setting, then a conflict develops, a plot unfolds in the narrative, and a resolution wraps it up. You experience the movie. The ending is the capstone of the theme.

Popular themes of recent films promote the "just look within yourself theme." The message is clear! Overcoming human struggles requires willpower, perseverance, courage, etc. The popular self-help themes seem to pale when faced with giants that cause fears and struggles. We are too weak within ourselves for spiritual battles. Like God's children at the Red Sea, we need help outside ourselves. Christ is our help and victor!

The battle belongs to the Lord. He doesn't say buckle down or keep your chin up, but find His strength in your weakness. So, yield weakness and trust Christ's perfect strength. Overcoming is not self-derived from human ingenuity or dogged determination but in the glory of another—the person of Christ. The enemy of your soul was defeated when Jesus died on the cross.

"Be strong in the Lord" is found numerous times in Scripture, along with "fear not." Many Christians never discover the great encouragement of Jesus' victory and resurrection life as strength. We become fearful and cave to feelings rather than renewing our strength in Jesus. We have an empowerment for victory in our battles. It is nothing self-derived but wholly of Christ.

When facing life's adversities, we become weighed down by besetting sins. Activities and attitudes outside God's will cannot offer ultimate satisfaction, meaning, and joy. All they offer is a momentary pleasure that leaves you with bitter consequences.

Habits of worry, anxiety, discouragement, fear, and dread keep us defeated. D-Day was a critical battle for the American and Allied forces as they stormed the beaches of Normandy under enemy fire. Estimates are that the average soldier carried 80 pounds of gear, the weight of water, and a barrage of enemy fire as they rushed the beach. They were facing the battle already weighed down. The writer of Hebrews encourages his readers to lay aside the sins that so easily beset us. They just weigh us down. We feel the crushing weight upon us while the enemy hurls flaming arrows at the soul.

Stand Firm

Half the battle of winning is standing. We find ourselves caving often too easily and quickly when faced with adversity. Paul reminds us that just like a Roman soldier has his armor, we are equipped with spiritual armor to suit up for the battle.

> Therefore take up the whole armor of God, that you may be able to withstand in the evil day, and having done all, to stand. Stand therefore, having girded your waist with truth, having put on the breastplate of righteousness, and having shod your feet with the preparation of the gospel of peace; above all, taking the shield of faith with which you will be able to quench all the fiery darts of the wicked one. And take the helmet of salvation, and the sword of the Spirit, which is the word of God; praying always with all prayer and supplication in the Spirit.
> (Ephesians 6.10-13, KJBT)

In Christ, we have the equipment to stand-spiritual armor that can withstand the darkness of the evil day. James tells us to draw near to God and resist the devil. Difficult days will arise, and the enemy will taunt us to scour in defeat. Jesus is your champion who stands before you.

Before a squire was honored with a knighthood, he kept a prayer vigil. With his armor before him, in silence, he contemplated the gravity of the daunting responsibilities. He gained spiritual resolve in an evening of Holy Communion, religious meditation, and considering his armor before him. Christ is our very armor, and communion with Him is our strength. Like the knight, our armor is complete. We lack nothing for a life of godliness and victory.

Let us consider our spiritual equipment for victory.

The Belt of Truth

The belt was a vital part of the soldiers' armor. The belt restrained his tunic and securely held the breastplate and the armor together. It was the foundation piece holding the armor together. The belt of truth is the foundation for spiritual victory.

Jesus guides us into truth. He is the way, the truth, and the life. Truth dispels deception, exposes wrong thinking, and discerns impure motives. Truth points us to the purity of God's Word and helps us rightly see ourselves and all of life. We fight against evil lies and distortions of the truth from the Evil One. The very core of our standing in Christ is truth. Truth simply anchors the soul in reality. God's truth is the "glue" for a life of personal integrity.

Breastplate of Righteousness

The Roman breastplate consisted of metal and leather. It protected the heart and all the vital organs in the torso. Christ is the believer's righteousness. Our "righteousness" refers to our right standing before God. Christ is our righteousness and protects the vitality of all our life.

The enemy attacks our emotions and sense of being right before God. He accuses God before our eyes and minds as we deal with adversity. The breastplate repels the arrows of Satan's assaults. Satan wants us to base our righteousness upon our performance. Our account before God stands good because of Christ's imputed righteousness. Christ's righteousness fortifies our hearts against the attacks from Satan.

Shield of Faith

The Roman soldier possessed a large oval-shaped metal shield made of layers of wood and leather or animal hides. He could completely stand behind the shield of faith. It was often soaked in water, which would put out the flaming darts. The enemy launched flaming arrows that intended to break down the structured formation of the soldiers.

The shield of faith defends us from insults or accusations that break down our faith and life. Without faith in Christ, we cannot please God. Faith means that we do not walk by what we see but by knowing the truth. The world walks by what is tangible, while the believer walks by a firmly rooted faith in Christ. Faithfully hear God's word and grow in faith.

Sandals of Readiness

The sandals were a half boot with leather straps and steel studded cleats. Proper footing was essential for Roman soldiers to keep formation and advance. The battlefield may be slippery and treacherous. The cleats gripped the ground and helped the soldier to stand firm. Soldiers remained ready for battle. Paul reminds us that the believers carry the Gospel of peace. Believer's "feet are shod" with the preparation of the gospel. In a world of evil, our feet must stand firmly on the foundation of the good news.

The gospel stands in stark contrast to the evils of this world. We stand ready to share the gospel. The shoes help to take the good news of forgiveness through Jesus Christ to those who need salvation. Satan wants us to think that winning people to Christ is unnecessary. We have a mandate and empowerment to share the message. Good shoes are essential for the journey. Witness the gospel of Christ in this war-torn world. Be faithful in the endeavor. You have the shoes for it!

Helmet of Salvation

A metal helmet protected the head of the soldier. It helped soften the blows of the enemy's attempt to decapitate them. The real battlefield is in the mind, how, and what we think. Our cognitive capabilities involve our thoughts, rationale, analysis, and the influences behind decisions and behavior. Our self-talk is the inward mirror we accept as truth.

Often, our half-truths and falsehoods shape our self-talk. The believer must intentionally fill his mind with the truth of God's word. Believing the truth of Scripture influences our behavior. Paul reminded the Colossian believers to "set their minds" on things above. Dispel the lying self-talk with the truth.

Sword of the Spirit

The sword of the Spirit was a short dagger secured by the belt. It was the only piece of the armor that was an offensive weapon. It is the word of God that breaks down man-centered thoughts and philosophies that control all of our lives. This piece of equipment helps the soldier advance in battle.

The short dagger was the soldier's weapon for hand-to-hand combat. The Bible is the sword that helps us advance in battle. Memorizing and meditating on the Bible empowers the believer to destroy the devil's works in our lives. While in His temptation, Jesus said it well. "Man shall not live by bread alone, but by every word that proceeds from the word of God." The truth of God's Word defeats Satan. Use it!

Conclusion

The believer's armor is always in front of him. There is no armor for the back because our marching orders are forward-moving. There is no room for retreat. Our champion is Jesus. His loins are girded with truth and righteousness, as He will return as the conquering King. He will be riding a stallion.

He is our victory and life. He is the first and last, the beginning and the end, alpha and omega. He who began His good work will complete it on that day.

We are more than overcomers through Him who loved us and gave Himself for us.

God has plans for the grace-gathering in the New Jerusalem. Far from the things that break our lives, His children will gather around His throne of love. The blessing of Communion around the banquet table will be glorious! Jesus will break bread and share the cup of blessing with His grace-gathered children. The grace-gathering, together forever, around the throne of grace! Until then!

God gathers up a community of the broken to make a gathering of the blessed.

~The Grace Gathering

Gathered for Genuine Care

Chapter Seventeen

Ephesians 6.18-23

In this Grace Gathering Series, we have discovered that,

God gathers up a community of the broken to make a gathering of the blessed.

We recognize that the community is called unto Christ, committed to faithfulness, a community of grace and peace, and "blesses the Lord." (1.1-3) This community is growing up together in Christ. This growth involves grace, knowledge, wisdom, and illumination. (1.15-23)

As His Body on earth, we are made alive, raised, and seated together. (2.1-10) This grace-gathered community is together as citizens of heaven, household, and new temple indwelt by the Holy Spirit. (2.11-22)

Together are members, heirs, and partakers. (3.1-12) These verses establish the theological significance of the grace community. Believers are empowered for a worthy walk in the Lord and in Oneness: Body, Spirit, Hope Lord, Faith, Baptism, God. (4.1-10)

The anatomy of such a church is a Christ-centered, disciple-making community, as a fellowship of truth and love. Bible teaching. (4.11-23), living out Christ's life in relationships. (4.25-5.2), especially marriage, family, and work (5.18-6. 1-4) round out the three final chapters.

The Family in Heaven and Earth

We discover that God has a forever family in both heaven and earth.

God means for you to be a part of it. Paul's letter to Ephesians succinctly describes the togetherness of the family gathering in heaven and earth.

Being "in Christ" is the theological center of Paul's doctrine of salvation and the church. His letter to Ephesians reminds believers that together they "are seated in heavenly places in Christ Jesus" in Ephesians (2.6), citizens' (2.19), fitted and built together in love (2.21-22), partakers (3.6), unified in the Spirit (4.3), the body of Christ (4.13), members of His body (5.30), believers who make supplication for all the saints. (6.18)

The church is a kingdom of light uniquely positioned in a broken world. Their message was God's gracious kindness extended in the gospel of Christ to everyone. This new community is saved by grace, sustained by grace, and grace shapes its very character. It is a community of grace-filled care. Soul care is at the heart of this community. What does this care look like?

In this final section of Paul's letter, we understand how such a caring community organizes. A church that seriously cares for the soul made it unique in the first century and even today. Christianity was an unrecognized religion in the Roman Empire, and there was much suspicion of this off-shoot of Judaism. Crucified like a common criminal, Jesus died a shameful death. His disciples were "unlearned" by the common social standards of the day. Many were slaves, and many were poor.

The early church did not have respectable temples or structures in honor of Christ. They met in numerous house churches, probably no larger than 40 people. At this point in the history of revelation, the sacred texts were being assembled. Ephesians is one such letter that made the canon of Scripture. They had the apostolic witness and teaching.

Love One Another

The first-century church was an authentic and caring community. Early church theologian Tertullian described the church that silenced many critics. Oh, how they loved one another. It was indisputable! A unified love remains a cardinal virtue of Christians. They will know we are Christians by our love. The song "We Are One in the Spirit" was right! Jesus makes us One in His love! They ministered to one another, body, soul, and spirit. They were a structured community of care. Church deacons' *diakonias* began for the physical care needs of widows (Act 6). Paul took up offerings and sent money to struggling congregations. Where the witness of the gospel flourishes, the value of human life rises in every way.

Early Christians formed burial societies to extend care to a pertinent community need.[1] I imagine they were also involved in bereavement care. Historically, the church has been at the forefront of humanitarian efforts, disaster relief, the establishment of hospitals, and the care of the poor, widows, orphans, and the homeless. Educational efforts led to the establishment of schools and training institutions. So, a literate culture can read and understand biblical revelation.

The challenge for the church today is advancing the gospel of Christ! Actively caring for one another and sharing God's love through the gospel is our central mission in the world. Look where lives are broken and ask, how can the gospel be applied in this situation? Let us look at what Paul lays out.

Interceding Care

An environment of Christian ministry is always in the context of prayer. The mode of operation for the Christian community is not dependent upon human creativity or hard work. Any success in the gospel is dependent upon the activity of God.

The uniqueness of the grace-gathering community is ministry to those facing spiritual battles. The grace gathering encourages people in all kinds of situations. The sectors of brokenness are ever before our eyes: addictions, substance abuse, divorce, health issues, sinful habits, broken relationships, dysfunctional families, gang violence, victim support, and the list goes on and on.

Believers compellingly stir up one another to good works and prayer. Prayer is our mode of operation, inviting heaven's will to be done on earth. The believer does not have armor to protect them in a retreat. The Christian life is always forward-moving. Prayer is the way to victory. Paul gives us the one offensive weapon in our spiritual warfare and how believers should pray for one another in life's battles. He encourages the Ephesians to pray.

---

[1] Bruce L Shelley, Church *History in Plain Language,* Thomas Nelson, Nashville, 2008, 35.

The season of prayer *kairos* means an opportunity. He gives a similar encouragement in 1 Thessalonians to *pray without ceasing*. Prayer is an invitation to God to work in our helplessness. An early 20th-century theologian, Ole Hallsby, said the best praying is "helpless praying." In other words, the battles of life are only opportunities to invite God to fight our battles. In these opportunities, God is most glorified.

Prayer is always in season in the grace-gathered body. It is always the standard mode of operation, as rightly revealed in the inception of the early church on the day of Pentecost. "Praying always with all prayer and supplication in the Spirit, being watchful to this end with all perseverance and supplication for all the saints." (Ephesians 6.18, KJBT)

Jesus even said that His house shall be called a house of prayer. He was doing more than naming the church but describing the vital life and breath of the church. The church earnestly prays and ministers to the care of others. Ministry is not in the context of vague generalities but specific supplications and petitions.

Prayer is a blessed way to express God's care. Troubles can leave you feeling alone and misunderstood. A community of prayer engages in empathetic listening and care and then carefully lifts specific concerns to the heavenly Father. Prayerful intercession is a ministry of unique caring. A caring church is a praying church. Prayer in the Spirit pursues the will of God and aligns with the Word of God.

Paul describes the qualities of such prayer with seriousness. It is watchful, intentional, and intense. A ministry of care is neither flippant nor casual. It cries out to the Lord for oneself and others. It humbly entreats' God to hear our prayers. It pours out from the depths of our soul, persistent in prayer. Perseverance means not giving up praying but remaining persistent and prayerfully pressing on. Praying for one another is the crucial ministry of sharing needs among one another.

Incarnational Care

Paul asked for prayer that he might be able to share the gospel as an ambassador for Christ. Even in his chains, Paul was aware of opportunities to share the message. Every sector of our society is hurting and broken. Where there is brokenness on a social level, there are opportunities to address the deeper prevailing spiritual issues with the gospel of grace.

Social needs are opportunities for planting the seeds of the gospel. Practical ministry opportunities build a bridge where the life- changing message of the gospel can bring life change. The gospel is the catalyst for the internal change. It lays a firm foundation for life to rise above the ash heaps of brokenness. Don't short-sell the importance of the message and your role in sharing the gospel in practical ministry to people.

Jesus' work was incarnational, as covered in a previous chapter. His ministry was shoulder to shoulder with people. He met people right where they were in their darkest despair and need of their souls. His life purpose was clear. Jesus had a message to declare as He read from the scroll of Isaiah in the temple.

> "The Spirit of the LORD *is* upon Me, Because He has anointed Me to preach the gospel to *the* poor; He has sent Me to heal the brokenhearted, To proclaim liberty to *the* captives And recovery of sight to *the* blind, *To* set at liberty those who are oppressed; To proclaim the acceptable year of the LORD. (Luke 4.18-19, NKJV)

The message of Jesus was both incarnational and missional. He came for the spiritually sick. Jesus came for those needing a physician of the soul, the broken, and those in the bondage of sin—the world, the flesh, and the devil. His message is redemptive, reversing the curse of sin for all time.

Paul sends Tychicus to them with his prayer request and communicates to them his condition. In the likeness of his Savior, Paul requests prayer for the mission. Paul observed all of humanity as a mass of brokenness because of sin. He prayed for opportunities to share the message.

> And for me, that utterance may be given to me, that I may open my mouth boldly to make known the mystery of the gospel, for which I am an ambassador in chains; that in it I may speak boldly, as I ought to speak. But that you also may know my affairs *and* how I am doing,
> (Ephesians 6.19-21, KJBT)

Paul gives a template for every mission-minded church. Paul prays for:
1. Gospel Opportunities in sharing
2. Boldness in the Gospel witness
3. Timely words appropriately spoken

Paul always looked to build bridges with his audience to gain a hearing. He became all things to all men, to win people to Christ.

Encouraging Care

Finally, Paul concludes the epistle by introducing the messenger. Tychicus is little known, but he played a massive role behind the scenes in Paul's apostolic ministry. His ministry would have been at a screeching halt if it had not been for faithful disciples like Tychicus. Paul strategically sent him to minister with the letter to all these churches in Ephesus on his behalf. What an honor!

> Tychicus, a beloved brother and faithful minister in the Lord, will make all things known to you; whom I have sent to you for this very purpose, that you may know our affairs, and *that* he may comfort your hearts. Peace to the brethren, and love with faith, from God the Father and the Lord Jesus Christ. Grace *be* with all those who love our Lord Jesus Christ in sincerity. Amen.
> (Ephesians 6.21b-24, KJBT)

Tychicus carried the parchment written by Paul. Remember, Paul wrote two-thirds of the New Testament. Tychicus was a letter carrier. His faithfulness helped shape the whole course of human history and Western culture. God uses little-known people for advancements in His kingdom. What if our work, ministry, or service is barely or ever recognized? Jesus rewards His faithful servant. Press on!

He was from Asia Minor and among the disciples accompanying Paul on his third missionary journey. He and the other men preceded Paul and waited for him in Troas. Paul describes someone dependable and trustworthy. He carried the heart of the Savior. Paul aptly describes four characteristics of someone with Jesus' passion for ministry.

Paul entrusted Tychicus with the care of souls and people's training and encouragement. Paul knew that he would do just that. Paul describes him as beloved. He was a well-loved and adored brother in Christ. He gained the trust of Paul and was very loved because of his empathetic care for the church.

Loving people is essential to have a ministry among people. Tychicus was simply authentic, and Paul sent him on a strategic mission of care to encourage the believers. He was faithful in duty. Like Barnabas, Tychicus would speak timely words of encouragement. Weary souls refreshed!

In his empathy, he came alongside those hurting and suffering, the discouraged and disillusioned. He could build them up in the Lord. It was a spiritual gift in the first century and remains one of the most needed gifts in the body of Christ today.

Whoever utilizes the gift of encouragement has numerous opportunities to minister. In a world of hurt, loving ministry is like a fragrant ointment for healing. Do you desire to be used by God? Pray for a ministry of encouragement and ask:

Jesus, give me your eyes to see people as you see them and your heart to love them as you love.

Pray it confidently. You might be surprised by what you see. You may be even more surprised by empowering love pouring through you. You can be Christ's hand and feet caring for the broken. Remember, you were once sitting in the ash heaps of brokenness.

We can safely sum up Tychicus' ministry with four outstanding qualities:
1. Empathetic Care
2. Faithful Authenticity
3. Purposefully Present
4. Comforting Encourager

His ministry began with empathy and integrity, and faithfulness proved His authenticity. Tychicus mastered the art of being purposefully present for them. He listened, asked questions, and he prayed!

Paul knew that once he got on the field with his letter, Tychicus would spring into action. He would represent Paul's tone and tenor before the hearers of this correspondence. Tychicus would give the right words at the right time. He knew that Tychicus had his heart for the gospel and deeply loved the Ephesian people.

Final Conclusion

Paul concludes the letter like he began the letter. The letter to the grace-gathered people was sent in the riches of grace wrapped in peace. In an uncaring world, many live with the harsh reality of love that has waxed cold. Sadly, many conclude that because suffering exists, there is either a loveless or powerless God, if there is a God at all. What a dreadful and sad conclusion.

God displays a church filled with gracious kindness. The church is present in the world to say that God is love. His power reaches into the dirty trenches of life. His hand reaches down in the dirt. His feet walk dusty trails. Like the compassionate Christ, His people have His heart for the broken.

An authentic faith lives out its love for God and others, and where love is present, grace and peace are close neighbors. It is not only a great ending to the letter, but a neighborhood of peace is a place to plant deep roots. Nurture gracious kindness in the gathering. We are on a mission of deliberate grace that seeks to rescue the perishing. God's family lives out heaven's reality on earth.

What a glorious reality and future awaits the Grace Gathering with unveiled eyes. Keep looking unto Jesus–the author and finisher of your faith. You'll behold His holy love and gracious kindness face to face. Until then!

Source Bibliography

Arnold, Clinton. *Zondervan's Exegetical Commentary on Ephesians*, Grand Rapids Michigan, 2010.

Barclay, William. *The Daily Bible Study, The Letters to Galatians & Ephesians*, Westminster Press, Philadelphia. 1958.

Brown, Colin. Ed. *The New International Dictionary of New Testament Theology, Volumes 1-3*, Regency Reference Library, Grand Rapids, 1975.

Burge, Gary M. & Green, Gene L. *The New Testament in Antiquity, A Survey of the New Testament within its Cultural Context,* 2nd Edition, Zondervan Academic, Grand Rapids, 2020.

Eerdman, Charles. T*he Epistle of Paul to the Ephesians,* Westminster Press, 1931.

Forlines, F. Leroy. *The Quest for Truth: Answering Life's Inescapable Questions*, Randall House, Nashville, 2001.

Jeffers, James S. *The Greco-Roman World of the New Testament Era, Exploring the Background of Early Christianity,* IVP Academic, Downers Grove.

Keener, Craig. *The IVP Bible Background Commentary of the New Testament,* IVP Academic, Downers Grove.

Meyer, Heinrich August Wilhelm. *Meyer's Critical and Exegetical Commentary on the New Testament,* Public Domain, Online Resource.

Nicoll, William Robertson. *The Expositor's Greek New Testament: Ephesians*, Public Domain, Online Resource.

Sergent, Gregory H. & Well, James M. Eds. *Retreat of the Soul: Reflection on the Contemplative Life by the Bardstown Brothers*, Hopeway Publishers, 2017.

Shelley, Bruce L. *Church History in Plain English,* Thomas Nelson, Nashville, 2008.

Simpson, E.K. *The Epistle to the Ephesians*, Wm B. Eerdmans Publishing, Grand Rapids, 1957.

Stowell, Joseph. *Ephesus: The Seven Churches of Revelation,* Our Daily Bread- The Days of Discovery, Video Documentary. (https://www.youtube.com/watch?v=JpJ-IWw5_Mc&t=750s)

Rogers, Cleon R. *New Linguistic and Exegetical Key to the Greek New Testament*, Zondervan Academic, Grand Rapids, 1998.

Thayer, Joseph Henry, *A Greek-English Lexicon of the New Testament*, Public Domain.

Tozer, A.W. *The Knowledge of the Holy*, Harper One, New York, 1961.

Vine, W.E. *Vine's Expository Dictionary of New Testament Words,* Thomas Nelson, Nashville.

Wright, N.T. & Bird, Michael F. *The New Testament in its World: An Introduction to the History, Literature, and Theology of the First Christians*, Zondervan Academic, Grand Rapids, 2012.

www.ingramcontent.com/pod-product-compliance
Lightning Source LLC
Chambersburg PA
CBHW020422010526
44118CB00010B/378